termite

By Suzy Pepper

ISBN: 0-9768304-1-8

Library of Congress Control Number: 2005902856

Printed in the United States by:
Left Hook Publishing
Houston, Texas
www.termitewatkins.com

This book is dedicated to:

Sharla – For being the best friend that I've ever had and for putting up with all the craziness over the years, and, most of all, for being the love of my life.

Tessa and Jared - For sharing their daddy with the whole world. You truly inspire me to keep going.

Mr. Mike Gfoeller and Colonel Steven Bruce – One man had the vision and the other chose me to fulfill it.

The United States Military – You protected all of us and lost many of your own in security Iraq's freedom.

The good people of Iraq – You welcomed me into your country and homes and entrusted me with twenty-four of your finest young men.

Acknowledgements

From Suzy:

Bailey Pepper – As the writer in the family, you inspire me to be my best. Thanks for the love, support, and humor you bring to our family every day.

Timothy Pepper – As the boxer in the family, thanks for the technical assistance. I couldn't have done it without you!

Doris and Jerry Chinnis – Thanks for always expecting the best from your kids, the premium you placed on education, and for loving your daughter.

Diane Chinnis Havens – Your support and love has been immeasurable. I couldn't ask for a better sister.

Gary Chinnis – Thanks for being there for everyone, Gary.

From Termite:

Bill and Wanda Watkins – For teaching me to always go for it!

Carla Watkins Black – Thanks for caring so deeply for me.

B.J. Watkins – Thanks for leading the way in supporting our country.

Bill and Gail McNeese – Thanks for your support, your love, and for your daughter.

Bobby McNeese – You were there for my family while I was gone – thanks!

Sharon and Connor Gains – For your love.

A huge thanks to the following:

The United States Olympic Committee – Without your support, it wouldn't have happened.
General "Buck" Walters – For being such a great leader.
Kenny Weldon and the Galena Park Boxing Academy – Thanks for opening your doors again.
Jim Hoeman – Thanks for your support.
Jay Wolfe – Thanks for making things happen in Iraq.
Najah Ali's parents –Thanks for bringing up an incredible son.
Mary Hancock – Thanks for your friendship and all your help.
Cliff Roberts and family – Thanks for hanging in there with me and for your advice and support.
Warmer Roberts – For your friendship and guidance.
To KBR friends around the world
To the great prayer warriors of Woodforest Church and Fellowship of the Nations – Thanks for all your prayers for my brother and me.

Introduction

This is the story of an extraordinary man. Termite Watkins met his boxing team in Baghdad at the height of the war. Many without shoes; none with even a mouth piece – most coaches would have seen desperation and hopelessness. Termite saw heart and opportunity. He wanted to give them what he had always taken for granted – the freedom to box.

Nothing about Termite Watkins is ordinary. Overcoming impossible obstacles became a daily existence for the new Olympic coach of Iraq. Where other coaches had years to get ready, Termite had fifty-seven days to turn this rag-tag group into an Olympic team. Building trust, bridging language and cultural barriers – finding a way became the team's mantra. He risked his life to keep their dream alive, at times entrusting weapon-laden Iraqi strangers as his escorts to practice. Regardless of how bleak things became, their eternally optimistic American coach stormed into the gym every morning shouting, "Iraq is back!" to his team.

Befitting the unique nature of this coach and team, the writing of their story came about in an unusual way as well. Unexpectedly crowned Iraq's Olympic coach, Termite wanted to tell old friends about this incredible sequence of events. Late that night in the military compound, he signed onto Classmates.com for the first time. Scrolling through names, he focused on an old friend he'd lost contact with years ago.

"Suzy," he typed, "You'll never believe what happened to me today. I just became the Olympic boxing coach for the country of Iraq."

Thousands of miles away in Atlanta, Georgia, I opened my e-mail and discovered a message from Classmates.com that Termite was trying to reach me. Friends since we were toddlers, there was an immediate comfort in being able to talk to him again. A rich history built from training wheels to proms bound us together so quickly that the gap of years diminished.

I became so passionately involved in the team's quest. E-mails flowed several times a day between Iraq and Atlanta. I was unprepared for one of them. "Suzy," it said, "You are the person to write this story.

A few of his e-mails frightened me. "Suzy," he wrote in March of 2004, "I don't want my family to know how much danger I'm in. If I don't make it out of here, please tell them how much I love them." Some of the correspondence frustrated me, such as the flurry of e-mails when the boxers got stranded at international borders and airports. Mostly, however, they inspired me, these tales of forgotten athletes who were being given this opportunity to represent their country in the Olympics.

Termite's story, in my opinion, is one of courage, perseverance, and character. Termite would tell you that it's just a story about people helping people. Either way, it's been a distinct privilege to tell the world about this extraordinary man, my friend, Termite Watkins.

"All they need is someone to believe in them.

I believe in them; this country believes in them.

I'm chasing a dream; they're chasing a dream,

and this country is chasing a dream."

Termite Watkins
Hilla, Iraq
October, 2003

1

Field of Daydreams

The youth baseball field throbbed with activity. Pickups parked right on the grass with their front bumpers nudged against the chain-link fence that stretched from home plate to left field. Every foul ball brought a moment of excitement as fans rose from their lawn chairs to see which car hood might get dinged by the ball. "That was a close one, folks," the announcer, situated on a wooden scaffolding behind home plate, would always say. Barefooted children raced over gravel and shards of coke-bottle glass to chase down the foul ball and receive a free snow cone as their reward. Little League mothers did their turn working in the stifling concession stand, frying corn dogs, pouring oil into the popcorn machine, and fishing dill pickles out of the huge glass jar.

Families lined up in webbed lawn chairs spraying OFF! on the legs and arms of their children. The merciless combination of heat and heavy rains made Houston a haven for the miserable pests, but everyone remarked that this year, 1966, was the worst year ever. Of course, 1965 was also called the worst year and 1967 would get the same status. All the children were dotted with bite marks, but they still played at the baseball field every night of the season. Wiry boys climbed like monkeys on the backstop fence, trying to race to the top before the umpire would swing around and growl at them to get down. Then, as soon as the umpire turned back toward the outfield, the scampering resumed at the same quick pace.

The field was in a huge square block in the shadows of the Houston Ship Channel that contained Cimarron Elementary School, practice fields, and basketball courts. Like a town square, it was the heart beat of a huge section of baby boom tract homes that were practically identical. Perpendicular

1

streets of neatly stacked small frame (and a few brick) homes each comprised of a single car garage, 3 bedrooms and one bath provided a comforting monotony. Hard-working neighbors arrived home from the paper mill or oil refinery to sit in front yards with ice chests loaded with Pabst Blue Ribbon. For at least eight blocks, the announcer's voice resonated. If a player struck out or missed a fly ball, the entire community knew about it.

The cadence of this area known as North Shore, although there was no shore for miles, had the regularity of tides. Waves of cars flowed out of the neighborhood and back in with the changing shifts of the local plants. Aluminum foil adorned the bedroom windows of some men working the graveyard shift. A certain respect was given these men; neighborhood kids knew to keep quiet when cutting through those yards. Hard-working men who spent most holidays working overtime expected the same level of effort from their sons.

"Termite!" a yell from the Texan dugout rang out. "Son, wake up out there!" Bill Watkins, coach and sponsor of the Texans was at the end of his patience. He'd sponsored the team, coached the team, and would probably have chalked the lines too just to see his son Termite field one good ball. Most of the coaches' sons were on the all-star team. His son had been moved from every infield position to the outfield until he was practically in the parking lot. "Every time I see you looking anywhere except at the batter is five laps around the field!" he chastised. His father's warning stung for a second but it was quickly pushed out of his brain by the excitement of the amazing firefly population that had taken over left field. Two pitches later, a routine grounder skidded past him. Pounding the chain link dugout fence with his fist, Bill's face became a series of pulsating veins stretching from his neck to his forehead. "Termite, for God's sake son, pay attention!" Bill shrieked.

Batting brought a short period of reprieve for the kid. At about half the size of the other players, the tiny strike zone posed a challenge to ten-year-old pitchers. The beer-gutted umpire struggled to get low enough to make the call. Fireflies and frogs settled in the far recess of his mind as fastballs flew at his head. Occasionally the ball managed to hit the bat, which made the game tolerable. More often, he got walked.

Bill Watkins watched his son run endless laps around the field at the next day's practice. As owner of Champion Exterminating, whose company name was sprawled across the team's shirts, it wasn't easy watching his son twirl around the outfield with no apparent talent for this sport whatsoever. As he watched Termite slug his way through his laps from his poor performance in the game, a worn out pickup pulled into the field with three boys hanging over the tailgate, two of which were twins. Sandy-haired and scrawny, Termite dressed, like all of the other boys, in jeans to avoid skinning knees in sliding practice.

As Termite wandered back to his permanent home in the outfield, Joe Dove emerged from his truck and tossed his beer can into the steel barrel trash bin buzzing with bees from leftover snow cone juice. Joe, just off his shift from Armco Steel, flipped down his dark sunglass lens over his safety glasses, and both men watched as Termite re-entered his own left-field world of blowing dandelion fuzz into the wind.

"Bill, have you ever thought about letting Termite give boxing a try?" Joe Dove asked. "My boy Randy and the Carr twins like it, and it wears 'em out good so they don't have any energy left for getting into trouble."

"Trouble," Bill thought. That's what he thought baseball would do – keep Termite out of trouble by giving him some direction in life. But, at the ripe age of ten, his son had already been caught smoking, drinking, and running a petty theft ring. Where would he be at twelve – doing hard time at Huntsville State Prison? Even on Sundays, Termite and the pastor's son at Woodforest Baptist Church were busy rolling tiny pieces of bubble gum and tossing them into the church women's sticky bouffant hairdos. Women would go home to their Sunday pot roasts unaware that Bazooka was in their

3

beehives until their husbands made note of it,or until their weekly wash and set.

Street fighting was Termite's biggest vice. He hated being called names; in fact, it was as if a switch clicked on his head when another kid called him "Stupid" or "Jerk," and if that name was a cuss word, the switch snapped right to rage. Termite had one strategy for kids who picked on him – fight them. Termite would then proceed to that child's door, ring the bell, and say, "Ma'am, your son just got his tail whipped because he called me a name, and if he says it again tomorrow, I'm going to whip him again." It was much like a thirty second public service announcement for the neighbors, except there was scant appreciation from the neighbors, who were left waiting for their bloodied-nosed son to arrive for dinner. Some of these fights took place right in the classroom, with teachers scampering to intervene. One minute, students were working quietly in their Big Chief notebooks, the next minute; a teacher would be pulling Termite out in the hall for a paddling. Termite fought his way to school, through school, and walking home from school; there was little doubt that this boy was heading for serious trouble.

Termite's problematic behavior was no secret. Bill frequented C & L Shoe Shine on Lockwood Drive in downtown Houston. The "C" in C & L was Clarence, Bill's childhood friend and Termite's godfather. The assets of the company consisted of thirty shoe-shine chairs in the absolute worst part of town, yet men of all rungs of the corporate and social ladder entered all day and exited looking down at shoes that reflected their images. It was a place where men talked. Joe Brown, former lightweight world champion, was a regular customer and heard the fringes of several conversations over the past months with the central theme being Termite's behavior problems. "Get the kid into boxing," Joe advised months ago, "And turn that street fighting into something positive."

The truth was, Termite modeled his father's behavior. The Watkins' children - Billy, Termite, and Carla had daily lessons in how not to behave. Alcohol mixed with a violent

4

temper plagued the home. Anyone who even faintly crossed Bill Watkins at the filling station or the grocery check-out ran the very real risk of getting beaten. In fact, Termite, from the window of his dad's truck, had seen his dad almost beat a man to death for a comment that others would have ignored. Bill Watkins' thin-skinned nature brought fiery tirades which were whispered about in surrounding homes, but the children in the house on Joliet Street lived with the constant worry of when the next explosion might occur. Termite looked at his father's refusal to take any guff off of anyone, and applied that knowledge to every classroom, playground, and street. He learned only one way to deal with conflict - hurt people.

The family's home life revolved around Bill's deep vacillation between Christ and scotch. Sobriety lasted for long periods of time, even more than a year, and brought positive changes in the family. When the church doors opened, all five Watkins were there. Bible meetings in the home, pot-luck suppers, father-led prayers around the kitchen table – they were the model of a Christian family. At times it was a bit intense, such as when Bill removed the television from the home for an extended period, calling it the "Devil's work." Overall, however, it was great, because Bill without the effects of alcohol was a wonderful dad and husband. The family rhythm was relaxed; no one had to worry about an impending violent tirade.

On a day like any other, that rhythm was shattered, without any foreshadowing of its coming. Bill's drinking engulfed him suddenly and completely – a bottle of Scotch a day mixed with milk accompanied with a steady stream of beer. Bible studies were cancelled and church stopped completely. As Wanda reflected, "Bill took his eye off God and turned it to man." The house on Joliet Street took on a dark hue.

The sound of his truck in the driveway no longer meant "Dad's home," it meant "Watch out!" The slightest irritation brought an unbuckling of his belt and lashings on the nearest son or daughter's legs. Liquor made him mean. His children paid for any comment made by a customer or employee hours earlier at work.

The family rode the binge out, but the costs were high. Welts on Termite's legs made him even more eager to fight every kid at school. When the drinking stopped and the church going began anew, it brought confusion in Termite's mind. Church was a place to go, to see friends, to play pranks on old ladies. Christ was in Bill's heart again, but there was no room for him in his son's.

Bill, seemingly unable to change his own destructive path, was determined that Termite would not follow in his footsteps. Finding a sport that Termite could excel in was his solitary solution to keeping him out of trouble, and now two men had advised that boxing might be it. Termite ran in from the field and, though he sure didn't know much about boxing, figured it had to be more fun than baseball. After all, the only time he came alive in baseball was when a fight broke out and the dugout emptied.

After practice, Joe Dove and the three boys met Bill and Termite two streets over at the Watkins' garage. Bill's garage was unique to the neighborhood. Needing space to store exterminating equipment, he had transformed it into a three- car garage that had more square footage than the family's small frame house. Termite's uncertainty about what exactly was going to transpire showed in his darting blue eyes – eyes that traveled from Bill, to Joe, to the boys, to an equipment bag.

Pulling the gloves out of the bag, Randy and the twins smelled blood. Termite pushed his small hands into the huge 16-ounce gloves, called pillows for their size, and shuffled his feet into the center of the make shift ring. "Time!" was called. Ronald, one of the twins, tapped his gloves together and moved in. Swinging his fists like a windmill, Termite was wide open. A brick slammed against Termite's right cheek. Stunned by the pain, Termite swung furiously to ward off the attacks. More and more punches landed on Termite's belly and face. Desperately, he tried to save himself and actually felt his glove hitting flesh on a couple of occasions, but Ronald just kept

6

punching him. Exhaustion set in after thirty seconds, and a panicked voice in his head asked how he was going to get himself out of this situation alive.

In the background, he heard Mr. Dove and his dad yelling instructions at him. "Get your hands up!" "Keep fighting!" The muscles in his small arms were so tired he could barely lift the gloves. Finally, "Time!" was called and the relentless barrage of punches ceased. Termite bit back the tears. He had too much pride to embarrass his father. His face pounded, but it was over.

Termite slumped against the garage wall trying to catch his breath, thankful that the ordeal was over. Lifting his head, he saw Ronald taking off the gloves and handing them quite deliberately to his twin who had a certain look of "Now it's my turn to kill him" on his face. Both twins outweighed Termite by twenty pounds and had ample boxing experience, but Rodney was the superior boxer of the two. Stunned by the fact that he had to endure this again, "Time!" was again called and sixty seconds dragged into an eternity as he tried to defend himself.

An onslaught of rhythmic punches hit their target – his face - he was sure that he was being beaten to death. He tried to recall moves that his older brother Billy had used on him, but the window in his brain slammed shut. Even the sounds of Mr. Dove and his dad were barely audible at this point. The only sound he wanted to hear was "Time!" His young body was aching and exhausted, and he made less and less contact with his opponent; his punches had no effect at all on Rodney. His opponent simply brushed them away like gnats buzzing near his face. The end of this sixty-second round left Termite disoriented and numb, and his brain did not want to face the reality of the pattern in place. There was still one more boxer to fight.

Time is a tricky thing; sixty seconds of resting seemed like a heartbeat. Sixty seconds of having the dog beat out of you was seemingly without end. Mr. Dove's son, Randy, had a reputation in the neighborhood as a tough guy and an excellent boxer, and was over a head taller than Termite.

Pain was replaced by fear as Termite saw Randy waiting for him in the center of the garage. Randy was a "head-buster", a term Termite would hear later in the boxing world. His cheeks, his nose, the sides of his head took blow after blow. Regardless of the beating, no matter what injuries he had to sustain, Termite refused to go down to the garage floor. He covered his face the best he could and took the butt whipping from Randy. When "Time!" finally rang out, Termite, at least relieved that Mr. Dove didn't have more boys in his truck, rested against the wall. After a few moments of silence, Mr. Dove proudly proclaimed "Bill, I think he will make it!" Termite wasn't sure what exactly he would make besides a punching bag, but his dad nodded in agreement.

Termite was unsure of his prospects at this sport. Baseball, for all the boredom it had for him, at least didn't get him killed. But the decision was made. He climbed into his dad's truck and they followed Mr. Dove on a fifteen minute drive to one of the toughest areas in downtown Houston. His face, chest, and arms throbbed as they drove in silence to a boxing facility called Red Shield gym.

Winos leaned against the outside walls of the Red Shield gym, where Termite was to be weighed in for a tournament the very next night. Billowing clouds of cigarette smoke poured out into the street when they opened the door; it was soon replaced by the smell of stale sweat a few steps later.

Termite took his place at the back of the long weigh-in line. Most of the other boys stripped some articles of clothing to lessen their weight; Termite kept his on to add whatever ounces he could. He could hear numbers being called out: one hundred ten pounds, one hundred forty-two pounds, one hundred sixty pounds. The Red Shield gym was primarily for underprivileged downtown kids to have a place to box, so it was mostly populated with teenage boys. But they were *big* teenage boys, and Termite's stomach churned as the line moved closer to the scales and he spotted the bloodstains on the canvas of the ring. "Name?" he was asked. "Termite Watkins," the voice cracked out. He held his breath hoping that he would not be asked the question he was always asked about the origin of his name. Red Shield gym was not the place to disclose that an exterminator who worked with his dad, when seeing the new baby at the hospital, remarked, "He looks like a little Termite." "Sixty-five pounds" was broadcast loudly as he stepped off of the scale. In reality, boxers just kept boxing. In his mind; however, it was the weight heard 'round the world. At least Termite was tougher-sounding than his given name – Maurice.

The next day, Termite played sandlot football all day long, but the thought of having a fight after the tail whipping he'd received in the garage was always present. After dinner, Termite and his dad headed for the gym for his first fight. There would be three rounds of sixty seconds apiece. Termite had the fresh knowledge of just how long three minutes of getting beaten was.

Arriving at Red Shield, Termite's stomach had settled to the point that he could look around the gym. There was one ring on the floor, metal chairs scattered about, speed bags, heavy bags, and kids jumping rope. Termite was handed gloves and a mouthpiece and told to go into the ring with his opponent, a Latino fighter. With no training to rely upon, he fought like he had on the playground at school, with wild, angry, windmill swings. Fortunately, his opponent had somewhat the same style, but still won the bout. After an unexpected win against the next kid who obviously hadn't had as much playground training, Termite faced the same Latino opponent who soundly beat him again.

Riding home from the third fight, Termite's head pulsated. Frustration welling in him, he looked across at his dad in the cab of the truck and said, "Dad, the only whipping I've ever gotten worse than that was from you. If I'm going to do this, I'm going to have to have someone show me what to do so that I don't get beat anymore." Bill nodded in agreement. Termite did not lose again for the next sixty-five fights.

2

Welcome to Iraq

The border between Iraq and Kuwait stood as an ominous warning to visitors entering from Kuwait. More than just a geographic tool separating two countries, this literal line in the sand separated the wealthy from the poor, the complacent from the terror ridden. On one side of the border, people who had barely caught their breath from the Iran and Gulf Wars were again struggling to care for families during a military operation and subsequent messy reconstruction. The prolonged agony of Saddam Hussein's reign had eroded the hopes of many of its people; they were in a survival mode, propping mattresses against windows to avoid incoming fire. In Kuwait, the other side of that line, it was life as usual. Streets of glittery luxury cars and window shopping in designer stores typified the lives of career-less Kuwaitis who relied on imported workers to provide services in their oil-supported welfare state. Wholly different existences were dependent on which side of the line a family lived.

Pulling up to the razor wire border, the sign said simply "Iraq" written in English and Arabic. The convoy of six black Chevy Suburbans carried employees of Kellogg Brown & Root (KBR,) a division of Halliburton, the main contractor in the reconstruction of Iraq. Each vehicle was equipped with a military driver and two "shooters," one riding shotgun in the front, the other in the back window. Termite's veins surged with nervous excitement. He was finally here, even if it was the most unusual pest control appointment he had ever had.

Getting to that point at that border seemed at times impossible. Termite felt compelled to be there, *drawn* to Iraq. The more he prayed for guidance the more the nagging, relentless feeling came; he knew he was supposed to go.

Explaining to his wife and best friend of twenty-four years that he had an overwhelming call from God to leave his six-figure car sales income and kill bugs in Iraq was a tougher sell than he had imagined. Relentlessly he cajoled, persuaded, begged, but Sharla was a hard sell. She told her husband, "I didn't get that call." She had been there during the boxing highs, but she had remained supportive during years of failed business ventures where vehicles were repossessed and homes were lost. No wife wanted to return to those days.

His first attempt to depart for the airport with KBR had to be cancelled due to Sharla's state of emotions. Termite could not get Sharla to stop crying long enough to say goodbye; she could not let him go. Day one of the inconsolable weeping was draining – by day three; everyone in the family was worn out. Termite was wholly committed to supporting America's troops in Iraq. Although he hadn't been in exterminating in years, he knew the business well from working with his dad and had overcome tremendous bureaucratic obstacles just to get his license rushed through Austin. Sharla knew that Termite's decision was void of any logic, but she also knew his level of determination. Resigned to Termite's insistence that he make a difference in Iraq, she sighed, "Termite, you can't change a country." Termite responded, "I know, but I can try. I can do my part."

The day before leaving for Kuwait, Termite made the goodbye rounds with tearful relatives. Bill Watkins, who had played such a pivotal role in building Termite's boxing career, had just suffered a stroke. Termite had to ponder, "Will I see my dad again?" His in-laws tried to muster support, but their eyes surrendered their bewilderment, "Let the military handle it," they cautioned. His twenty-year-old daughter Tessa just hugged her dad and whispered "Daddy, I love you." Jared, his grown son, squeezed Termite like it was the last time he would see him. No one in his family comprehended his passion for going, but all were certain that there was just no stopping him. But he was here now at the border, not just the border of a country; he was crossing a line into a new chapter of his life.

11

The shooters in each Surburban scanned overpasses and scrubby trees for the enemy as they sped through the southern Iraqi desert heading for Umm Qasr. Nervous about an altercation with their foes, what they encountered twenty minutes from Kuwait was quite different.

Entering a town, the convoy stopped reluctantly at an intersection. From the shadows of the hot desert, a parade of shabbily dressed children appeared and quickly descended upon the caravan. Their small fingers clung to the side mirrors while they balanced on the sideboards of the vehicles. They all had the same plea, "Water, mister, water, water." Their unwashed faces pressed against the middle passenger seat, meeting Termite's eyes. Some jumped in front of the caravan in an attempt to force the drivers to stop. They all repeated the mantra, "Water, water, mister." Termite's driver, accustomed to the routine, swerved sharply to shake the children from the Suburban and accelerated to over 100 mph. Small brown bodies wobbled away from the convoy as the billowing dust clouded behind the vehicles. Termite could not swallow. From the young age of sixteen, he had delivered countless speeches to Houston area schoolchildren about hard work, discipline, and the American dream. As a young man, he felt so called by Christ that he'd tried to save the world one person at a time. Yet here, he could not provide a cup of water to a child. Security concerns of children placing grenades inside car windows prevented any actions to help them. Termite's sense of mission deepened.

The KBR convoy was delivering a variety of skilled workers to support the military in readying a military base in Umm Qasr, a port city located about two hours from Kuwait. That support could mean wiring lights, killing snakes, building a toilet, or cleaning one. Their supervisor had warned them that a contentious general was threatening to sue KBR if they didn't get there quickly and rid the camp of bugs *today*. Termite's energy level, always high, just percolated now at tackling his first assignment. He had made drastic, upsetting changes to his family's life to be there, but it felt right.

12

Termite straightened his 5'8" boxer frame, cleared his throat, and walked into the former port offices to meet the general. The general was Roger "Buck" Walters, a fellow Texan who had surrendered a comfortable retirement to oversee the reconstruction in the southern provinces of Iraq, which extended from the border of Kuwait and Saudi Arabia to just north of the city of Karbala. Umm Qasr, at first glance, was a fairly typical port city with cranes and grain elevators etched on the horizon and railroad tracks crisscrossing the warehouse buildings. Termite's second glance was a constant reminder to the danger the workers and military were in; sand barriers rising above twenty feet were constructed around the camp to provide protection from incoming artillery. No ships were docked, and the only Iraqi workers there were those recruited as laborers by the U.S. and British military just weeks after capturing the port.

General "Buck" Walters was dignified in appearance. Slender and gray-headed, he looked more suited to a corporate boardroom than a stifling desert office. Termite's eyes jumped down to the loaded, cocked pistol in the general's holster, military type vest, and desert boots. "I'm supposed to check in with you, sir, about your bug problem," Termite introduced. Saturated with sweat from the 125-degree day, the general looked sharply up from his desk. His frustration with KBR's sluggishness in getting someone out to take care of the pest problem so his men could get a decent night's sleep had simmered to the boiling point. He was about to kill the messenger. "Yes, you are. And if you don't get rid of these f---ing flies, I'm going to send your f---ing ass back home and I'm going to file a breach of contract with KBR."

Termite was stunned into silence for several seconds. He was not going to be reprimanded like a ten-year-old by anyone. A hailstorm of thoughts rained down on him: saying goodbye to his family, quitting his job, his mother-in-law's advice, "Let the military handle it, son." He wasn't expecting balloons on his arrival, but he sure wasn't anticipating getting chewed out by a general before even having an opportunity to prove himself. "Sir," Termite tersely replied, "I did not give you permission to cuss me; so therefore, I'd appreciate it if you wouldn't." A simmering pause ensued, as Termite tried to keep his rarely seen temper in check. He knew this was a general, he knew he risked being sent back home, but his verbal counterpunch flew anyway. Termite, from his earliest memory, got a certain knot in his stomach when people called him names or used profanity at him. He felt the words he rarely used coming to his brain; he'd had too long of a day for the censor to kick in. Termite looked squarely in the general's eyes and returned sharply, "I'll tell you what, if you let me get my f---ing ass to work, I'll get rid of your f---ing flies." As Termite pivoted to leave, the general shot off, "You're full of piss and vinegar – aren't you? You'd *better* get your butt working." Termite got to work.

The general's "Welcome to Iraq" speech was not the most motivational one he'd ever heard, but Termite quickly refocused on finding a way to get rid of the meanest, most aggressive flies he'd ever seen without any chemicals. Securing rolls of screen from a KBR carpenter, Termite replaced the windowpanes in the entire office with screens and added a screen door to the general's building. The intense heat combined with the diving flies made Termite more sympathetic to the general's foul mood. Within twenty-four hours, the flies were gone and the temperature in the building was more bearable. He hadn't conquered the world, but he had made the general happy, which, despite their tense introduction, was important to him. Smoothing over their rough start, the general joked that concentrating on work was much easier without the constant worry of being carried off by the flies.

After a tough first day with the general, Termite stretched out on his cot under the Iraqi ski, sweat drenched from the 110-degree evening temperature. Reflecting on his family's daily routine, which, with the nine-hour time difference was just beginning, he would dream the same dream in a war zone as in his soft bed in Houston. At night, he was always a boxer. On good nights he was winning; on bad ones he was cut and bleeding, but still fighting.

14

The KBR employees adjusted to the rhythm of working eighteen-hour workdays in a Spartan setting. For KBR, meals for the first week were military rations, eaten in whatever spot gave some element of shade. The Iraqi workers, however, brought their lunches, packed in square clothes tied at the four corners. Walking by the group of Iraqi's with his ration bag, one of the few English-speaking workers invited, "Mr. Termite, come eat with us." Termite watched the men empty their food offering into a big pile in the middle of the circle. Reaching with bare hands, the men would eat the mixture of foods, swatting flies away from the banquet. Enthusiastically, he took a seat among the men and dined, offering a small portion of his rationed water to each man. They were the first to ask the same question he would be asked throughout Iraq: "Are all Americans like you?" "Well," said Termite, "Some are like me, some are a whole lot better than me, and a small percentage is just bad." Relief spread across the men's faces.

Termite spent his early days making arriving soldiers' homes livable by ridding them of rats and two-inch deep pigeon dung. It was tough work, but somehow rewarding knowing that a U.S. soldier would benefit by having a decent place to sleep. He figured that's what General "Buck" wanted too – a decent place for the soldiers and coalition staff.

Preparing to work one morning, a British colonel barked at Termite, "Who are you?" Reluctant to have another curt exchange with anyone, Termite politely replied, "I'm your pest control guy." "Are you any good?" the colonel abrasively asked. "Yes, sir," Termite replied. Trying to have a simple polite exchange, Termite inquired, "I hear your accent, where are you from?" Obviously irritated, the colonel sarcastically answered, "I'm British, can't you tell?" Becoming increasingly annoyed with this conversation, Termite sniped, "If I could tell, I wouldn't have asked." The colonel continued, "Why do you ask?" Pausing to reflect on his encounter with the general, Termite tried to avoid another confrontation, "Some great boxers have come out of Britain." The colonel looked at the exterminator and asked incredulously, "What do you know

15

about boxing?" Termite looked deep into Colonel Bruce's eyes and announced, "I know everything about boxing." The colonel followed, "Have you ever boxed?" Termite replied, "Yes." Colonel Bruce queried, "Were you any good?" Termite continued the eye contact and said, "I was the best." The Brit continued, "Have you ever trained anyone?" Termite explained that he had trained some of the best in the U.S. The edges of the officer's sharp demeanor softened a bit from a tough colonel to an everyday guy interested in boxing. "Meet me on the British side tomorrow at 5:00 A.M. and we'll see how good you are," the colonel challenged.

At 5:00 A.M. the next morning, Termite walked the short ¼ mile stretch toward the port waters to meet Colonel Bruce, not knowing whether this was for a workout or a personal challenge. The two men shook hands in the dark and talked about Colonel's Bruce's training expectations. A hammer man whose job was to keep a tight clamp on operations, one-on-one he was a man of tremendous personal warmth. With the backdrop of the Iraqi port, the men stretched their muscles. Termite showed the colonel how to hold his hands properly, and the two men shadowboxed in the relatively cool, 95-degree morning. The forty-ish Brit was already in tremendous shape, but he wanted to learn to box. Their heavy bag, the only equipment they had, hung outside from a welded frame. Here, in the most unlikely of gyms, Colonel Bruce and Termite, a novice middle-aged boxer and his pest control teacher, worked out together each morning at 5:00.

Being the colonel's personal trainer in the morning was the best part of his job; the worst part was working at the Enemy Prisoner of War camp (EPW) near Umm Qasr. Just the heavily armed drive to the EPW was harrowing, much like NASCAR with AK-47's. Drivers routinely drove well over 100 mph in order to avoid being hit by missiles or gunfire. Every maneuver was employed to avoid coming to a stop, the most typical being driving in the opposing lane until just before a head-on collision and then sharply veering back.

16

The EPW was not a traditional prison of bars and concrete. It was a makeshift prison in the middle of the desert constructed of twelve-foot tall razor wire that stretched for acres. No floor or roof existed, just razor wire sections with a small tarp in the corner for shade. The prisoners ranged from Saddam Hussein's Fedayeen to common criminals to men who were captured during the invasion who would be released fairly soon. In these razor wire walls, up to 7,000 men and teenaged boys were crammed like cattle in a holding pen.

To enter the prison, the workers had to go through a series of zigzagged checkpoints designed to slowly weave cars through stops with tanks or machine-gunned topped Humvees. After finally arriving at the entrance, Termite walked past a few freshly dug graves of prisoners who had attempted to incite a riot. Inside, he had an inkling of why.

Each razor wired section had a parallel trench, another row of wire, and a guard posted at each section, making escape a very remote possibility. Inside each rectangular area existed deep pits around ten feet deep. A plywood sheet with bored holes covered the pits. These were the prison bathrooms, and they were brimming over with human waste. Some of the pits that had reached their capacity were simply left open and pests of all kind hummed around the pits. Walking through the overcrowded prison, the stench from the massive human waste mixed with severe heat was at times physically unbearable. A week ago, Termite was selling cars. This week he was trying to control the spread of disease in an area while prisoners were defecating and urinating right in front of him. The Brits were in the process of handing control over to the Americans, and the troops were doing their best, but the best there meant food cooked in an area covered in flies in an environment not conducive to even keeping food down. The prisoners were given a blanket and, weekly, a small amount of water for washing; the prison soldiers lives weren't much better in the early days of the war. Termite ordered the full bathroom pits bulldozed and treated the prison the best he could on his visits

17

there, but he refused the request to work there overnight. He simply could not.

After only a couple of weeks in Umm Qasr, General Walters asked Termite to join a crew heading to Hilla to prepare the camp for the Coalition Provisional Authority (CPA.) After their initial harsh exchange, Termite had quickly developed a tremendous respect for the man and was anxious to do the very best he could for him. He made a promise to General Walters that his new office would be vacant of vipers, scorpions, bees, and mostly, those intolerable flies.

Nine hours north of Umm Qasr, the city of Hilla lay in sharp contrast to the southern port's bleak desert floor. Hilla's topography boasts a combination of desert sand juxtaposed with lush carpet of lime green grasses and more date trees than any other spot in the world. Just as fertile in history as in land, the ancient city of Babylon is situated just one mile away. The biblical accounts of Daniel and the lion's den, King Nebuchadnezzar and Shadrack, Meshach, Abednego, and the fiery furnace took place in the shadows of Hilla in Babylon.

The men were exhausted from working twenty hours in the Umm Qasr heat. After a few hours of sleep, they packed the eight Suburbans for the drive to Hilla. Termite and John Hauck, his site supervisor, attached a trailer for storage and positioned sixty gallons of gas on the roof for the trip, since the chances of getting gas were, at best, uncertain. Most of the vehicles had shooters; theirs did not to the large number of supplies they were transporting. The Suburbans headed north, and John positioned their vehicle in the middle of the caravan for protection. Quickly, all the drivers accelerated to a pace of 125 mph for the long haul. Termite settled into the middle seat of the Suburban, and Halid Grozdonic, an administrative person with KBR, sat in the front passenger seat.

Initially, a mood of quiet nervousness permeated the car. Every overpass had a potential for danger from the enemy, and the enemy was hard to discern because they were often in civilian clothes. Forty minutes of edgy nerves rolled into hours of just trying to stay awake, much less alert. The road varied from two lanes to one, but no shoulders were adjacent to the pavement - there was just a sharp drop off of about four inches on each side. They traveled quietly, each partly reflecting on their week, partly battling much-needed sleep. They would arrive in Hilla in less than an hour.

The hum of the whirling tires against the pavement lulled all three men. Termite unbuckled his seatbelt and gave up his fight to stay awake. His head bobbed until it rested to the side in a deep sleep. Halid fell into slumber. Unfortunately, so had the driver. A shrill scream rang out from John, and Termite and Halid's heads popped back quickly. When John's heavy eyes had finally succumbed to fatigue, all four wheels of the Surburban had slid off of the road. Desperately trying to maneuver the Suburban back onto the highway, the wheels hit the lip on the side of the road and the vehicle started flipping. The momentum catapulted Termite to the third seat where he straddled the broken window. His legs and hands were situated on each side of the window as he watched the road and the sky tumble by. Frantically, he tried to hang on, but almost lost his footing, nearly falling to the road. The screeching sound made by metal hitting pavement rang out over the desolate desert. The Suburban rolled three or four times before coming to a rest on its side. When the tumbling vehicle finally stopped, Termite exhaled, "Thank you, God!"

It was the shortest prayer that Termite would say that day. Feeling a searing heat, a quick blink down disclosed that his shoes were on fire and flames were dancing around his body up to his crotch area. "The fuel tank!" Termite gasped to the other men, but no one responded. Climbing out, a sharp pain rang in his shoulder, and he struggled to pull himself out of the window. He stomped the flames out on his feet and quickly assessed the situation, which looked unmistakably bleak.

John and Halid were still in the Suburban amid the burgeoning flames. Termite had to do something before the sixty gallons of fuel blew. On his knees, Termite pounded on the vehicle close to John, screaming desperately for the men to get out. Termite could see the flames encircling John's listless face. Termite struck the car over and over with his fists shrieking, "John, Halid, get out! Get out!" Termite rotated to the other side of the vehicle and his fists continued the rhythm against the burning car as he pleaded for the men to get out.

Frantically searching his brain for any plausible game plan, Termite attempted to enter the flaming Suburban to pull the men out. A shaken Halid heard Termite's cries of, "Give me your hand! Give me your hand!" Halid reached up to the window above his head, as flames rose in front of him. Halid released his seat belt as Termite encouraged him, "I'll support you, Halid." A mangled, bone-exposed hand surfaced. Termite grabbed it and pulled Halid out of the Suburban, which was more than fifty percent in flames. As members of the convoy began arriving, Termite moved Halid to a safe distance from the blazing vehicle.

Returning immediately for John, the fire had virtually engulfed the SUV. He watched the fire crawl over John's face. Termite again struck the car and begged continually, "John, get out!" Termite dove back into the fire and began climbing back into the vehicle. John's head twitched with movement as he resumed consciousness. Grabbing him, he pulled John from the flames and guided him to Halid's side.

As Termite bent over to catch his breath, the explosions began – only four or five seconds after pulling John out of danger. The men retreated to a safer position and watched the Suburban explode into a ball of fire on the open desert. Sitting on the side of the highway, John's bloody head leaned into Termite. He whispered, "Termite, I've never been much of a believer or anything, but did you see what I saw?" Termite replied, "What did *you* see, John?" John paused and weighed his response carefully, "Something held the flames back until we could get out." Termite turned his eyes back to the Suburban and nodded. He had seen it, too. "John," Termite answered, "That was the hand of God."

An army helicopter arrived to medivac the men to a medical unit just across the Kuwaiti border. Hamid's hand was so badly damaged that he had to return to the states for reconstructive surgery. John's head wound was treated and he was released. Termite's shoulder suffered a torn rotator cuff and would require surgery back in the states, but it could wait until he came home to Texas. He was determined to keep his word to the general that he would take care of the bugs in Hilla before his arrival. Later, the general would just chuckle and shake his head at this crazy Texan who had to be coaxed onto a helicopter because he didn't want the general to be carried away by flies.

When Sharla received Termite's call from the tent hospital, the sobbing began. But this time the cries were from Termite, not Sharla. "I know that God has a purpose for me here in Iraq," he confided, "I know that you think I can't go around changing countries," he continued, "and I know that I can't do everything alone, but I know that I can make a difference" Sharla responded, "Termite, you are exactly where you are supposed to be; I know that now."

Just two weeks had passed since he had quit his job, left his wife and children, and said goodbye to his parents and in-laws. He was just days into the new chapter of his life, trying to make a positive contribution in a war-ravaged country. What would the next page of his life bring?

3

A Champ in the Making

Galena Park in the late 1960's was rusty and worn; a working class town on the literal edge of the Houston Ship Channel. Fittingly named for an old oil company, refinery flames and holding tanks consumed Galena Park's landscape. The evening hours, with the twinkling lights of the ships and industry on the channel, concealed the daytime reality of the aging steel mill and corroding public works. Tougher and labeled more redneck than neighboring North Shore, people who lived in Galena Park saw it as a nice community; those who just passed through impulsively locked their car doors. A close knit community, Dement Field, the only high school football stadium in the area, packed in the crowds on Friday nights, especially when their beloved Yellow Jackets faced their rivals, the North Shore Mustangs.

Kenny Weldon was comfortable in Galena Park. Born and reared there by his single mom, he was focused on saving enough of his boxing earnings to open a gym in the town. A lanky twenty-one year old featherweight, his professional record of 5-0 was just the jump-start he needed after years of impressive boxing in the amateurs. Like many other nights, he was headed downtown to referee a fight and to promote his upcoming bout with whatever small crowd was there.

His destination, the Salvation Army Boy's Club in downtown Houston, turned its gymnasium into a boxing arena every couple of months for local youths. They assembled a floor ring with padding under the canvas and set up chairs around the ring. Kenny had just finished refereeing a fight and was talking boxing with a small group as Termite's bout commenced in the ring. Kenny observed the skinny youngster's street-fighting manner for a minute, shook his head from side to side, and proclaimed to everyone in earshot, "Boy, this kid is bad!" After a second glance and further reflection he added, "But he sure does like to fight."

Bill Watkins' search for the right man to train his son would hopefully end that night. His discussions with Joe Brown at C&L Shoe Shine had led him to Kenny. "There's a kid out in Galena Park who's a heckuva boxer – see if he can help Termite," Joe offered.

In close enough proximity to overhear the exchange about his son's lack of talent, Bill moved a few steps closer to Kenny, "That's my son, and, you're right, he's bad right now. I need someone to train him and you might be the right guy." Kenny was taken aback. He had never trained anyone before, and although his brain was an encyclopedia of boxing fundamentals, he was reluctant to take on a little kid with not even the sheerest element of basics who would siphon time from his budding professional career. Filling the empty conversational space, Bill inserted, "Look, he doesn't know much now, but he wants to learn." Sensing Kenny's lack of enthusiasm, Bill continued to sell the idea, "Listen, I've got to find something that Termite can do well, and it's sure not baseball or football. He's getting into fights four, five times a week, and I'm thinking, the kid likes to fight, let's teach him the right way to box."

A winded, beaten Termite joined the men, excited about meeting a professional boxer. It was tough to square Termite's angelic face and contagious smile with what he'd just heard of his troubled behavior, but he liked the boy immediately. Not having a dad in his life, the level of determination on the part of Bill Watkins to straighten Termite out struck a chord with Kenny. "I can pay you $125.00 a week," Bill induced. Kenny liked the challenge and he needed the money. "We'll start tomorrow," replied Kenny. A man who would later train Evander Holyfield was now responsible for teaching a ten-year-old novice everything he knew about boxing.

Driving the five-minute trip in his 1958 Buick Wildcat from Galena Park to North Shore, Kenny affirmed that the coordination Termite needed would have to be developed the hard way. Awkward and clumsy were the two adjectives that came to Kenny's mind describing the kid, not good descriptions for a boxer. Kenny pulled into the driveway of the small, green frame house on Joliet Street and found Termite waiting in the yard for him with his bag packed for the gym.

Calling Termite over to the driveway, Kenny began. "Termite," Kenny explained, "In boxing, everything starts with the feet, so we have to get your feet doing the right thing." An intent eagerness to listen and learn marked Termite's facial features. "Before we go to the gym, I'm going to show you some drills that I want you to do every single day." A crack in the concrete delineated the driveway from the garage addition – the perfect place for Kenny's demonstration. Staying on the balls of his feet, Kenny hopped from one foot to the other with the line in the center of his body. Termite tried with less than impressive results. "That's good," said Kenny. "Practice that, but try to get into a rhythm; boxing is about having a rhythm." Termite nodded. "After you get that down, work on this." Kenny went back to the line and, with his hands on his hips jumped with both feet back and forth across the line." Termite stumbled through it. "Not bad," fudged Kenny, "but keep your body centered over the line."

The downtown gym housed a variance of talent, sizes and ages. It was a unique learning environment in which a heavyweight George Foreman trained in close proximity to a tiny kid from North Shore. The guy who ran the place, Shifty Dandio, treated everyone the same, with a gruff "What you want?" greeting upon entry. An old boxer with cauliflower ears, a big, pounded-in boxer nose, and an absence of teeth, his oversized shoes superceded the other features to Termite. Being a curious child, Termite focused his eyes on his shoes and got a quick, "What you want?" Kenny explained that when boxers left their towels at the gym, Shifty kept them and rented them out to other boxers for fifty cents. The money he made was stuffed in the open spaces of the shoes, but he frequently pulled the cash out, flashed it in boxers' eyes, and repeated his tired saying about boxers hanging on to their money, "If you got a little gold, you can be sassy and bold, but when you're broke, you ain't nothing but a joke." Older guys were used to Shifty's negativity and threats of "I'm running you out of here," but to a new kid, Shifty took some getting used to.

Termite took Shify literally and thought that he might get "run out of here," so he followed Kenny closely through his new training regimen, which was built around strict time constraints that mirrored boxing rounds. In this manner, a boxer's body and mind developed around expending energy and power in rounds, not random times. Shadow boxing to warm-up was first for three rounds of three minutes with rests in between. Termite then sparred for three minutes or worked with Kenny utilizing hand pads. Rounds on the heavy bag followed to develop punches. The crazy bag, a small leather bag suspended by cables above and below it, built hand-eye coordination, timing, footwork, and rhythm. Termite's favorite speed bag was next that developed rhythm and coordination. Jump roping concluded the workout – a skill so lacking for Termite that Kenny simply looked elsewhere. Awkward and clumsy were still words in Kenny's mind, but Termite's ability to listen and process information impressed him.

Arriving back at the Watkins' home, Termite was exhilarated, but exhausted. Kenny turned off the ignition, looked at the boy, and said simply, "Now, we run." Just down the street from the Watkins was Greenwood Park. Consisting of saggy-netted tennis courts, a baseball field, a gravel parking lot, and see-saws and swings, the two ran the perimeter a few times. Kenny studied Termite's unnatural running technique, but couldn't make sense of it. A great deal of movement with legs and arms, he was definitely churning up the air, but he didn't go anywhere. "Heel, toe, heel, toe, he called out to Termite, but things just got choppier. "Later," Kenny thought.

Kenny backed out of the driveway with a genuine fondness for the boy. He had purposely tested Termite's physical limits to gauge his motivational level, and he could not have asked for more effort from his new student. Termite watched Kenny drive off knowing that this day had forever changed the course of his life. Up to this point, he had been good at nothing except getting into trouble. He was so proud of the day he had just had. His mother Wanda called him in for dinner, and then Termite went to the crack in the garage and practiced his line drills for most of the evening.

The next morning, Termite awoke early with a slightly smaller chip on his shoulder. Standing on his bed to view his tiny frame's reflection from the dresser mirror, he shadowboxed. Somehow, his tiny muscles seemed a bit bigger today. Slipping through the house, he went to the crack. Over and over he drilled, until his mom called him in for breakfast. Throughout the day, the sound of his teacher's voice at Cimarron Elementary droned into a haze of thoughts about boxing. He could not wait to get home – back to his line in the garage – back to the downtown gym to workout with Kenny.

The drive time on Interstate 10 downtown became his teacher's lecture hall. Explaining to Termite the "sweet science" of boxing, the art of hitting without being hit, he learned the difference between punchers and boxers. Kenny talked to him about concepts such as exposing the least amount of his body and getting into position to punch. Just as much class time expired over methods utilized to avoid getting hit as Kenny spent on punching techniques.

Termite studied the professional boxers at the downtown gym. Etiquette at the gym dictated that when a pro wanted to use a bag, the amateur stepped aside. Termite loved standing near them, watching their fists sink into the heavy bag. He then emulated their techniques as best he could. After his workout, he carefully observed the pros sparring, especially Manny Gonzales, a welterweight who had the tremendous ability to hit and not be hit. Boxers in the gym referred to his style as "beautiful." *"That's* a boxer," Kenny emphasized. He watched a different type of fighter, Raymond Boyd, "The Pink Panther," deliver one tremendous punch for a dozen received. A puncher with a then undefeated record; the "pink" part of Raymond's nickname came from his pink boxing robe and trunks. The fact that he put his foot on the chests of his knocked-out opponents and growled like a panther provided the rest of the name. After studying both styles, Termite wanted to be a boxer; he liked the idea of hitting without getting hit. He was unsure about the growling part.

As the weeks progressed, Termite started rising at 5:30 A.M. for his road work, but with a new menu that included backwards running, throwing punches while running, bobbing and weaving, and skipping. In pitch-black darkness, Termite ran miles around a neighborhood that soundly slept. He was obsessed with training – the runs got longer and the gym time later. The crack in the driveway became a twenty foot long duct taped line where sneakers hit the concrete hour and hour establishing his rhythm. Every weakness he attacked by relentless, constant practice. He now had the dream and the energy to stay the course and a young teacher to direct him.

He won. Fight after fight, week after week, adorned in his blue trunks and sequined robe made by his grandmother, Termite won. Time after time, Termite set up opponents with his left jab – picked them apart with the jab – then stopped them with his left hook. Joe Brown was now training Kenny, and Termite's exposure to Joe's training methods elevated his proficiency. Joe affixed a rope across the entire width of the gym at about four feet tall, and Termite crossed the gym repeatedly, bobbing and weaving under the rope. He learned to move in the corner with the sole purpose of getting his opponents to throw a punch at him, then he would side step them, throwing them into the ropes, and finish them. A right-handed fighter, Termite's weapon was his left. The more he won, the harder he trained. After winning twenty in a row, Kenny struggled to even find opponents willing to get in the ring with him.

Just eleven, a call from a promoter quickly bumped Termite's boxing status up to a new tier. Termite would be the first amateur on a pro card in Houston's Sam Houston

Coliseum. Accustomed to fighting in front of gym-sized crowds, the opportunity was immense. Having been a fight spectator at the coliseum many times, Termite was accustomed to buying a ticket, going through the gate, and finding a seat. The thrill of going through the fighters' entrance at the side door in a dark, smelly alley was immeasurable. Sharing a dressing room with professional fighters, taping his small hands next to theirs, putting on his robe stitched with a sparkling "Termite Watkins" on the back – the boy treasured every second.

The coliseum was grander than ever that night, and the crowd cheered louder and louder for the kid who could move and punch like a pro. The more they applauded the bigger show he gave – he unabashedly loved the attention. After his win, Ray Collins, a famous sports writer for the Houston Post, interviewed him. The next morning, Bill Watkins picked up his paper in the driveway and, opening to the sports section, read an article entitled, "A Champ in the Making." Termite looked up from his line drill in the garage and grinned.

Six days a week, the grueling boxing schedule consumed his focus. Roadwork began now at 5:00 A.M., followed by school, homework, and the gym for several hours. Termite had to be home at 8:00 and in bed by 9:00 seven days a week. The Watkins' family routine adjusted to it. Bill relocated the exterminating equipment from the garage and constructed a boxing ring in its place to make training more efficient. Winning sixty-five fights in a row, he was so well known in Houston that one fighter described Termite's home field advantage as "fighting in his living room." He was so stirring to watch that in one fight coins rained down on the ring from fans so appreciative of the effort. Fighting every weekend involved constant travel to and from cities in and out of Texas and a quick return for Monday morning classes.

By junior high, his clean-cut image and big smile earned him the distinction, The "Donny Osmond of Boxing" by a reporter. He was, without a doubt, the only boxer whose mother ironed his hand wraps and workout clothes.

The temptations of junior high for other students bypassed Termite as he continued to master the art of hitting without being hit. While other parents searched rooms for pot in 1969, Termite's parents, concerned about weigh-ins, rummaged under his bed for hidden M&M's that he concealed throughout his room. Fights at school had practically stopped, except for a boy who just could not resist calling Termite "Turdmite" on a regular basis. Throughout class, this kid continually whispered, "Hey, Turdmite." Waiting for the teacher to turn to write on the board, Termite walked over to his desk and busted him right in the face, and then calmly sat back down. Termite had seen every principal's office in a five-mile radius, but this time he was a little more contrite when the paddle stung his behind. Knowing he could fight well inside the ring somehow lessened the desire to do so outside of the ring.

Wanting to learn from other trainer's methods in addition to Kenny's, Raymond Boyd, "The Pink Panther," briefly joined their team. In total contrast to Kenny, who was low-keyed and maintained strict decorum in his behavior, Raymond had attitude. After all, this *was* a man who bellowed like a panther over his knockout victims. Rough, tough, and wild, his joy over a well-connected punch was contagious. He didn't have the science of Kenny, but he sure spread the love of fighting and made Termite a more aggressive puncher.

That preparation contributed to a huge win in Dallas against a bigger, older, Golden Glove champ. The victory came against a fighter who Termite should never have faced. Arriving in Fort Worth, his scheduled opponent couldn't fight, and the only substitute was seventeen-year-old Richard Lord. A hometown favorite, Richard Lord adamantly opposed fighting Termite; in fact, he said he would not do it. "I can't fight him, he's just a little kid." he goaded. Termite's father heavily advised Termite against the fight. "Son, he's more experienced, and he's in a higher weight class," Bill cautioned sternly. The decision came down to Termite. Raymond's view was "Get in there and get him." His fourteen-year-old pride won over his common sense, "I want to fight *him*," he said, pointing a finger at Richard. Bill's reluctance continued, "Termite, you need to stop and think about what you're doing." His son's blue eyes were filled with determination, "Dad, if you don't let me get in the ring with him, I'll quit fighting." It was a tough, hard fought fight, but Termite prevailed. In later years, his stubborn pride would cost him.

The demands on Kenny's boxing career brought to a temporary end the close relationship between Termite and his mentor. The new trainer in his life was Albert "Potato Pie" Boulden, nicknamed by Joe Brown for his love of sweet potato pie. Where Kenny was a great boxing teacher; Al was a technician. Not a boxing specimen himself at 200 pounds and 5'8" tall, he was a master at what it took to win. His instructions were highly specific, such as "Get your shoulder up one inch, Termite." A stern motivator, Potato Pie took no back talk from any boxer, and workouts were no nonsense. Famous for saying, "When you can do it, call me," and walking away when a fighter balked at his directives, any reluctance on a fighter in following instructions vanished quickly. Termite knew that if he did exactly what Potato Pie said, he would win, and he did. Potato Pie's approach was comprehensive, he kept his boxer focused, rested, and highly motivated. The combination of his coach's attention to details and Termite's ability to process information effectively brought the now 135 pound high school student to a new level of skill.

High school for Termite contained few dances or late night toilet papering parties. Roadwork now started at 4:30 A.M., and where school ended, practice in the gym began, followed by dinner, homework, and exhaustion by 9:00 P.M. The higher the level, the greater commitment he gave. The greater the obstacle, the more enjoyment he gleaned from overcoming it.

Even when love bit Termite, it was with a girl content to place his boxing schedule above her social desires. Linda Kelly, a delicate-looking brunette, spent every afternoon in the gym, not scrutinizing the moves, just waiting for small breaks to talk to him. Termite treasured the fact that Linda was there and labored even harder to impress her. Fully cognizant that boxing was his life, it quickly became hers. Everywhere Termite went, Linda went, from church to the gym to media interviews, Linda's quiet sweetness filled his heart. Everything was right. He had the girl, he had the focus, and he had the skills developed by six years of total devotion to a sport.

And he had Christ. On an average Sunday in an average month, Termite went to church. The Watkins family was on a non-church going cycle now, so he accompanied Linda to her church. Termite had been to a million services just like this one; in fact, he'd probably heard close to the same words spoken by a plethora of pastors. None of the words held much meaning for him. He had simply gone through the motions of standing for hymns, sitting for sermons, passing the plate, and heading for the door.

Until today. The pastor wasn't particularly charismatic, nothing spectacular in his presentation at all. That morning, the words were just for Termite. "Where would you go right now if you died, heaven or hell?" the preacher asked, "If you answered heaven, why?" Termite felt sure he was the only one in church that day; the words were just for him. There was no congregation around Termite; he was alone. He felt suddenly inspired to have a personal relationship with Christ. It was the biggest day of his life, bigger than any fight. Sitting in the pew, he made a deep commitment to Christ. Something happened to Termite that morning – he made the decision to let Christ into his heart.

Every single day, he read the Bible, absorbed the words. Termite was so exuberant about his new-found faith that he wanted everyone to know about it. His position as a top fighter gave him the forum he needed. Youth groups, civic clubs, at school – Termite took every opportunity to spread the word of Christ. He felt a deep, personal responsibility to touch lives, to be a messenger for Christ.

Termite was ready mentally, physically, and spiritually for the fight of his life. Each and every one of those finely tuned skills and positive mental state was required in the 1973 state

Golden Gloves tournament. Fighting several times throughout the week in one tough fight after another was physically draining. Termite drew on the hard-earned experience of over eighty amateur wins and relied on Potato Pie's constant motivation to defeat opponent after opponent. The finals were an awesome display of precisely honed skills of spinning his opponent, left hooks, and right-left-right combinations. Tremendously confident from winning the state tournament in Fort Worth, the training began for the Golden Glove National Tournament in Lowell, Massachusetts. Kenny was uneasy and advised Bill and Potato Pie that Termite was too young for the nationals. No one had won it at sixteen and he would have to fight much older opponents. Termite knew he was ready.

Winning the Texas state title underscored the fact that this kid was on the cusp of a big boxing career. But he was also a high school kid struggling to fit in like everyone else. There had always been two realities for Termite. In boxing circles, he was highly regarded and admired, often staying late to sign autographs after his bouts in the coliseum.

However, on most Monday mornings, Termite would arrive at North Shore High School, bruised and swollen, and few asked why. Well-liked at North Shore High School, he wasn't particularly popular or even nominated for "Most Athletic" because he did not play the sport of the state – football. Sports pages contained his picture almost every week, and adults appreciated his work, but since he wasn't featured at pep rallies or in morning announcements, he was just the average kid. It was stupid, but it bothered him. Every Thursday night, the girls from the high school drill team decorated the football players' yards with signs and ribbons for the upcoming game with prolific thoughts like "Squash the Bees." Every Friday, students missed academic time to cheer wildly for a football team that rarely advanced even to regionals. Their glorification continued into Friday nights, where everyone converged at Dement Field in Galena Park to watch their favorite football stars. Few from high school, except his girlfriend Linda, actively supported his career.

Until now. The morning he left for the nationals, he awoke to find signs and ribbons crowded in his yard. "I'm like a football player," Termite reflected. Pulling onto Uvalde Road, the main street in North Shore, signs were everywhere, mostly saying, "Good Luck, Termite!" Leaving North Shore, down Interstate 10, all the way to Houston Intercontinental Airport, Dairy Queens, muffler shops, and dry cleaners had removed the weekly specials and replaced them with words of support - so much encouragement for a boy who'd found his rhythm centered over a crack in the driveway.

The Golden Glove team boarded the Boston-bound plane for the national tournament with the state trainer in tow. Termite needed Potato Pie in his corner for the series of tough fights – Al's aggressive strategies and strong motivational techniques kept him focused. Termite's temperament had mellowed so much by high school that one reporter described him as "docile," but Al knew how to get him ready to fight. Potato Pie and Bill drove from Texas to be there.

For four days, the Texas State Featherweight Champ boxed. Everything he'd been taught in the gym for six years he used. Poised and confident, he fought tougher and older fighters throughout the elimination process. After winning the championship fight, he did something he'd never done. He dropped to his knees in front of the crowd and thanked the Lord for getting him there. Holding up his trophy for the crowd, Termite clutched with his other hand a jacket with National Golden Gloves Champion on the back. Finally, he had a letter jacket to wear back in North Shore that surpassed those of the football players.

Entering his senior year as the youngest national champ ever, Termite continued his demanding training schedule. He fought three grueling fights against Mike Ayala, another national champ from San Antonio, and won each of them in different venues. He qualified for one of the five U.S. Olympic teams with Sugar Ray Leonard and Howard Davis, topping off the tremendous roll he was one. Traveling to Europe representing his country, Termite felt such pride walking into an arena with the Olympic jacket on his back.

After the European tour, he returned to Texas in the midst of a political mess. Growing numbers of amateur boxers were disgusted with the distribution of funds by the Amateur Athletic Union (AAU), the ruling body of boxing. Boxing brought in money for the AAU, and boxers were tired of those funds being allocated back into swimming and other programs, while they went without needed equipment. Termite and other boxers decided to take a stand against the AAU, and boycotted their events to force a change. Additionally, the boxers formed a competing boxing organization called the Good Gloves and set up tournaments. The AAU, in retaliation, suspended boxers, including Termite, for fighting in unauthorized fights. * After months of political bickering, Termite realized that the only arena he could not win in was a political arena. Disillusioned with the politics surrounding amateur boxing, he announced that he would fight his first professional fight two days before his high school graduation. At age seventeen, with an amateur record of 118-10, he would enter the next arena as a professional, giving up his dream of going to the Olympics, yet excited about tackling the new challenges ahead.

*In 1978, two years after the Montreal games, the U.S. Congress passed the National Sports Act, which addressed the distribution of funds in amateur sports. Boxing, from that point, governed itself. Unfortunately, many frustrated boxers who protested the workings of the AAU had left the sport. Their commitment to addressing these issues; however, strengthened amateur boxing for future athletes.

TERMITE WATKINS

4

A Fighter by his Trade

Termite was in hostile territory. The clamoring of the crowd in Miami Beach was not for him. Potato Pie and Bill knew his adrenalin level was particularly high, because the boxer slept soundly on the locker room bench. His trainer had seen this behavior before in athletes when they were fully primed and didn't take it as a bad sign. The excitement of the packed house swelled as time grew closer for the main event; they could hear it through the thin locker room wall. Thirty minutes remained before the symbolic touching of the gloves would signal the start of a ten round battle, and their nineteen-year-old, baby-faced warrior slept.

The extra dose of adrenalin, along with executing a perfect game plan, would be necessary to beat not just Juan Hidalgo, but also his master trainer, Angelo Dundee. Famous for being in Muhammad Ali's corner, Angelo Dundee cultivated champions, and the crowd's anticipation centered on Dundee's new protégé pummeling Termite. Both boxers were undefeated as pros, Termite with twenty-one fights under his belt – Hidalgo thirteen. Both had classy boxing styles, with the tremendous ability to move and punch. Both were extremely conditioned and well prepared. Hidalgo, however, had two advantages: a harder punch and the hometown advantage, exacerbated by the fact that Angelo's brother Chris was the promoter of the fight.

Less than two years after turning pro at seventeen, Termite's quest to be a world champion was on track. The transition from amateur to professional had been interesting. His father was now his manager, his high school girlfriend his wife and the first five opponents knocked out in early rounds. Potato Pie escalated his conditioning to adjust from four to ten round bouts. Paydays weren't too impressive – his first fight with an unknown opponent grossed him $600.00, but the money got better. Bill postponed taking his cut until the Termite Show got rolling. A phone call from a promoter with a bizarre matching of karate masters and boxers brought the biggest sum to date. Nationally televised the next day, the peculiar night would burn into the memories of fighters, fans, and the Houston Police Department.

Heavily hyped, 1975 was the first time the two realms would meet, and for good reason. The karate masters predicted a virtual slaughter of the boxers. Termite was the first boxer in the ring, ever, in this type of match. After deflecting kicks in the first round, Termite knocked Chong Lee out of the ring with a left hook in the second. Lee's handlers pulled him back into the ring and propped his listless body on the corner stool. One minute into the third round, Termite hit forceful punches to the Korean's chest and knocked him out. The second bout was worse for the Koreans, when Gene Wells dropped the karate master in the opening round. When Mike Quarry entered the ring for the third bout, the frustration peaked for the Asian fighters. Mike's punches immediately connected, and his impotent opponent relentlessly head butted Mike in desperation. The ref's terse warnings went unheeded by the Korean, who continued defying the rules. Bewildered fans watched the karate fighter position himself against the post of the ring and repeatedly bang his own head against it in apparent punishment for his performance.

Termite, already dressed after his short fight, sat ringside and watched the Korean's self-infliction of pain in disbelief. After smashing his own head, Young Tae Lee pulled nails from his martial arts glove and scraped Quarry's legs, which immediately oozed with blood. Termite was unwilling to wait for the ref to see the offense. He took off one of his typically 70's high platform boots and slung it at the Korean, popping the fighter right upside the head. A mêlée ensued, with a dozen boxers and karate fighters in the ring. The Koreans pulled their swords, signaling Termite, the boxers, and the panicked promoter to head toward the exits. The Houston police sorted out the mess and a showdown in Texas over the toughness of the two sports concluded with angry patrons demanding refunds, police intervention, and a boxer arriving home with one boot. It was a most unconventional, yet profitable, night for an up and coming fighter.

The Hidalgo bout *was* a conventional fight; however, and every ounce of training and conditioning in his 135 pound body would have to be summoned. Easily roused by his dad, Termite knew what he had to do, and those in the locker agreed. "I've got to make Hidalgo come at me. If he starts coming at me, he'll get off his fight, but I'll stay on mine." After Bill wrapped his hands, Termite stretched, rubbed his muscles with a mineral oil combination, and shadow boxed, using the punches he planned on bringing to the ring.

Termite entered the ring in his purple and pink robe to dotted disingenuous applause and a few boos. Juan Hidalgo, the Dundee brothers' next Ali, rocked the house upon his entry. Termite was nervous. It was a fight between two equally talented fighters, but it was also corner against corner. He hit and moved, but so did Hidalgo. It was a struggle of such similar styles and talents, two boxers peaking at the same moment, that the smallest degree of quickness and mental toughness made the difference. Termite stayed on his game plan, forcing Hidalgo to be the aggressor. With Termite's early point advantage, Hidalgo had to come after him. Great at deflecting the left hook, Juan's defense broke down on the second and third left hooks. Termite's skill at spinning opponents into the ropes got Hidalgo turned around. Both were great boxers who clashed relentlessly from bell to bell, but Termite counterpunched to a huge victory. The man groomed to be the next champion lost to an exterminator's son whose only dream was to bring the World Championship to Houston. He was a huge step closer to that dream.

The next bouts were early round knockouts against lesser opponents. Termite traversed the country by car, driving seventeen hours straight to Albuquerque for a second round knockout. He broke attendance records in California, Texas, and Florida cities. Sports pages reiterated his wholesome representation in the toughest of sports, saying his demeanor was more suited as an altar boy than a fighter. One paper went so far as to say that his boyish smile clashed with his violent profession. Termite saw no conflict; indeed, he respected this sport and had no problem knocking a guy out on Saturday night and going to church on Sunday morning. Some sports writers described his skills as "complete" and "pure." Another distinguished him as "far too fast, far too clever." He was a white boxer, an oddity in itself, with perfectly styled hair, an easy laugh, and the ability to make everyone around him comfortable in liking him.

Whatever words were selected, anyone who watched him fight knew two things: he loved the audience's reaction to him and he loved fighting, because fighting was what he did well. He was, however, tired. He'd put a lot of miles on his 1970 GTO working his way up to the opponents he needed to beat to get a title shot. The boxer hit towns praising his opponents and left the city limits criticizing his own performance, regardless of its flawless nature. In his eyes, he was never sharp enough, hadn't trained hard enough, or hadn't capitalized on every opportunity in the ring. The rhythm in training boxers to hit their peak right at the opening round was critical, and Bill and Potato Pie worried that their boy needed rest.

Bill wanted to cancel the fight. Nani Marrero was heavier, fighting in his hometown of Miami, and had an awkward style that could bring trouble. The thought of canceling the fight brought out the same obstinate will Termite exhibited in the Richard Lord fight at age fourteen. Bill heard the same threat from the past, "Dad, I'll quit fighting right this minute if you cancel this fight." After all, he was 25-0 – he could beat anyone. The trainer and the manager's concerns were brushed aside by an invincible nineteen-year-old attitude.

The Miami Herald article the next morning opened with this summary: "Termite Watkins found out how to lose Tuesday night, and he found out the hard way." A broken

39

knuckle from the second round diminished his right. A bad cut over his left eye from the fifth that Marrero continued to counterpunch marred his vision. Blood streamed from his face. At one point, Termite threw a roundhouse that missed with such force that he fell to the canvas. Awkward and clumsy, his rhythm had left him for the night. The partisan crowd loved seeing him get beat; the Houston television stations interrupted regular broadcasting to announce the lost. The golden boy had gotten whipped.

After a three-month hiatus from boxing, Termite packed for the road, healed and restless to fight again. He watched the Montreal Olympics unfold, with Sugar Ray Leonard and Howard Davis, and checked his bottom dresser drawer to be certain the unused USA warm-up was safely stowed. He'd seen so many arenas since the days he and Howard and Sugar Ray played checkers late into the night in Europe. A four-round bout with protective headgear was ancient history to him. He was a pro with a manager, trainer, and a wife to support. He clicked the suitcase hardware and headed first to Biloxi, then on to New Orleans, and finally Corpus Christi.

Termite brought his 27-1 record into Corpus to fight twelve rounds against a tough boxer, Rocky Ramon. A stocky puncher, Ramon was a talker, telling Termite the morning of the fight, "Take it easy on me, I'm not in good shape." Termite knew how it worked, the mind games boxers played on their opponents. As Termite carefully smoothed the Vaseline on his face, Ramon burst into his dressing room. "Watkins, if I don't knock you out by the third round, I will do whatever it takes to take you out." Termite chuckled and rolled his eyes.

Termite's superior skill level overwhelmed Ramon during the first two rounds, landing five punches for every one attempted by Ramon. The third round opened with a continued thrashing by Termite. Desperate for a win, Ramon planted his head firmly under Termite's jaw and jolted his head upwards with all of his force he could muster, breaking the hinges on Termite's jaw. Ramon's threat in the dressing room rang true. The bell sounded signaling an end to the third round. Bill angled the corner stool between the ropes, sat the boxer down, and tried to remove Termite's mouthpiece, but Termite swatted his hands away. He couldn't open his mouth wide enough to remove the mouthpiece. Incoherent mumbling came from the boxer's mouth, but Potato Pie saw the swollen hinges. The trainer and manager agreed, "We'll have to stop the fight, Termite."

Angry about getting into a position long enough for Ramon to head butt him, furious about ever conceding a fight, Termite's speech was gargled, but everyone saw the determined eyes and knew the threat, "Dad, I'll stop boxing if you stop this fight!" The three looked at each other. The bell sounded. Potato Pie shrugged and advised, "Son, then you'll have to go out there and box and move." For nine rounds, Termite held his right fist in front of his jaw for protection. Termite used his strength and experience, spinning Ramon into the ropes and onto the floor. The twelfth round sent Ramon to the floor with a right-left-right combination. The fight ended as Termite's celebrated left hook dropped Ramon to the canvas as the last bell sounded. After the bout, Ramon offered a critique of Termite to a reporter, "He's good, but he's a dirty fighter."

The fixation to win a title was the constant in his life. He'd accumulated other titles: Southern Lightweight Champ, the Texas Lightweight Champ, the Golden Gloves National Champ, but he needed to break through to the next level. Termite kept fighting - good fighters, mediocre fighters; they primarily came to *his* hometown now. Selective in facing opponents who had straightforward styles, Termite continued to build his record by fighting his fight, and rose in the lightweight rankings, waiting for his shot at Roberto Duran. He relied on his sidestep, his hook, and Joe Brown's early advice to "Use the left hand and keep the right one cocked."

The twenty-year-old fighter's focus on boxing on his terms, fighting his fight, unraveled in frustration against a celebrated Golden Glove champ from Indianapolis, Norman Goins. Two great boxers met in the ring, both resolute on fighting their styles, both determined to succeed at any cost.

Goins was a great puncher – out of twenty-five professional fights, seventeen of his opponents were knocked out; Termite was too illusive to knock out.

A passionate fight from the opening bell, both men spoiled the rhythm of the other. Goins had such ring-savvy that he made every part of the ring work for him. He cut the ring off, took Termite's jab away, and immobilized his spinning maneuvers. Termite, however, was so hard to hit that Goins' benign punches were without impact.

Frustration mounted as neither capitalized on their strengths and competitive tempers replaced thoughtful game plans. Norman elbowed Termite repeatedly; Termite repaid him. Termite's eyes stung from the illicit thumbing; Norman's were just as red. The disintegration of the match continued despite constant referee warnings and attempts to pull the men apart. Two highly respected, finely tuned fighters were in a street brawl, palming, holding, and lacing each other.

Both boxers knew the dirty moves, and Termite was more proficient than most. The seams, laces, thumbs, and even the horsehair stuffing could be manipulated to hurt a fighter. In the past, Termite used them judiciously to strike back against opponents who used them, much like a pitcher evened things up in retaliation for a beaning. This fight was different in Termite's mind. Norman's instigation of this type of a fight, and the continuation of the tactics called for reciprocation on his part. Bells signaling the end of rounds pealed and neither boxer halted; the ref surrendered any power to keep them apart as the rounds rolled by. Bill's pleas to "Box, Termite, box!" were drowned out by the Texas crowd's shouts of "Get him, Termite!" The officials disqualified both boxers, who each received a "no decision" for the bout. Respective handlers jumped to the center and stood between the boxers. A match more suited for a liquor store parking lot ended without a winner. Termite had no regrets; he did what he had to do. He simply could not back down from a challenge.

The buzz surrounding a possible title fight between Termite and either Roberto Duran or Esteben DeJesus intensified – his job was to stay ready. At 37-2, he continued to polish his physical skills, particularly his roadwork, because, despite every trainer's best efforts, he was too sluggish, averaging only eight minutes per mile. To get to his feet, he attacked his mind.

He didn't just study Jose Silva's methods of mental preparation and visualization - he encompassed them. Affirmative statements scrawled on 3 x 5 cards sang out from every bathroom mirror, car visor, and cupboard door. "I can do this!" was the mantra repeated in his brain. He re-read passages of Silva's book before running or fighting. Roadwork got longer and faster, he continued to push himself past any normal distances for boxers. His mental transformation allowed him to focus on his stride and overcome fatigue and pain. At 4:00 A.M. Termite ran eleven or twelve miles around North Shore with an average per mile time of five minutes and forty-five seconds.

Unfortunately, a supply truck full of 3 x 5 cards could not bring him what he so urgently needed. He was in eternal limbo for a title shot. Termite's focus kept his boxing sharp, with no losses during 1977 or 1978. Fighting mostly in Houston and Florida, some bouts ended before the crowd got settled, such as a knockout against Rick Craney who fell in the first minute and a half as one reporter quipped, "Like a sack of flour." Craney's response: "I've never been hit harder." Other nights, his game wasn't perfect, like when an unheralded Joe Medrano knocked Termite on his tail in the first round, but Termite quickly recovered and knocked the fighter out in the seventh. Ranked ninth, Termite waited for the chance to win a title, but the stipulation from Don King and Duran was that Termite would have to agree to a sum of money that was demeaning, roughly 1/20 of Duran's payday. As Termite told a reporter, "Unfortunately, I can't fight for the featherweight or the junior welterweight title either because King has them tied up too." His dream of bringing a championship to Houston dimmed.

At twenty-two, his perpetual optimism seemed inextinguishable. Speaking to students across the country, he communicated the importance of overcoming obstacles, and his "Glass half full" philosophy of life. Before fighting in Madison Square Garden against Teddy Osuna, Termite visited a school in the Hell's Kitchen section of Manhattan, and told the junior high audience, "If we become quitters just because things don't go our way, we'd never get anything accomplished." Students heard of his training regimen ("I can out jump rope any girl here") and his habit of getting to bed by 10:00 each night. He interwove the importance of education, work ethic, and the critical element of respecting teachers. Termite always included the fact that he was a Christian. He wanted the toughest guys in the audience; the guys dressed in black jackets in the back of the auditorium, to know that being a Christian didn't mean a man was weak.

His own teacher, Potato Pie, greatly inspired and motivated Termite to continue pushing himself towards his dream. The love between the trainer and the boxer was well known in boxing circles –when Termite got hit, so did Potato Pie. Tremendously confident in his corner, Termite trusted Potato Pie's guidance through matches, and changed strategies solely on his recommendation without the slightest hesitation. Everything Potato Pie said, Termite did, and he won as a result of his guidance.

Termite was also devoted to his dad, the man most singly responsible for him even having a career. No one spoke of the conflict simmering between the two men; Potato Pie was just suddenly and inexplicably gone. Under the brave, boxer's veneer, the fight in him diminished hearing the news that his trainer for ten years had left. Boxing would never be the same.

Losing his beloved trainer came at the worst possible time. His record of fifty-two wins and two losses was being challenged in the biggest clash of his career to date. Howard Davis, Olympic Gold Medallist, and Termite Watkins, who walked away from the Olympics to start a career, were the two highest ranked lightweights in the United States. With Termite ranked 6th in the world and Howard ranked 10th, there was little doubt it would be one heck of a fight, but it was so much more. The winner would stand alone as the best lightweight in the United States, and be completely deserving of a title bout. Davis had incredible speed in his hands and feet, was 11-0 in his pro career, and had trained particularly hard on punching power. Termite's training in the fall of 1979 could best be described as erratic and confused.

Bill brought in top-notch trainers for advice, but there were too many competing voices, too many approaches, and too many tactics. Tony Gardner, one of the new trainers, knew Termite's camp was "grasping at straws." Tony advised everyone in earshot to "Keep the kid on the same training; don't change a fighter who's been so successful." Stronger opinions about how to get the boxer over the final line to a world title bout overshadowed Tony's common sense. Harder punching, quicker feet, less road work, more roadwork: the game plan shifted from workout to workout. His natural style now seemed unnatural; well-intentioned trainers tried to transform a boxer into a puncher. Termite disclosed to a reporter, "We're working on three different styles for the fight. We won't know which one we'll use until the bell rings." In a far recess in his mind, Termite, the man who willed things to happen by positive thinking, doubted if he could win without Potato Pie; worse, he questioned whether or not he still had the zeal.

Publicity swarmed around the upcoming match that potentially could make one career and break another on the same night, and was aired on CBS's *Sports Spectacular*. As Pete Ashlock, a promoter who did the matchmaking for the bout said, "It's Termite's pro experience against Howard's gold medal." Termite thought the world of Howard as a fighter and as a friend. Both dignified, neither engaged in baiting or talking down opponents in the media, and this fight was no exception. At one press conference, one of Howard's managers forced a can of Raid on him to use as a prop against Termite, and Howard became visibly uncomfortable with the stunt. Termite announced, "Raid won't kill Termites and that I ought to know because we've been in the pest control business all my life." Termite emphasized that they were old friends from the Olympic team, and, after handling business – the fight – they would return to being friends.

Howard Davis, a vegetarian who easily made weight, was astute about one point in particular – Termite struggled to make weight. A clause in the contract penalized him $10,000 per pound over weight. Making weight for a boxer can be an excruciating process, and this was no exception. Termite did his roadwork in nylon sweats with only sparse, carefully measured water to extinguish his thirst. He chewed gum to induce salivation and then spat into a Dixie cup and measured the ounces. Food intake was rigorously restricted. Still not at weight, the boxer worked up a good sweat. One of the trainers took a rolled-up towel and scraped his body of all water and oils. Baby powder was applied and another scraping ensued to get every drop of oil. This provided the last ounce needed and prevented a financial and mental loss right before the fight. Losing ten pounds in two days took a mental and physical toll; his body was pushed to perform at a high level while his brain screamed for water and food.

His normal routine with Potato Pie would be to eat lean protein and healthy carbohydrates before a fight to regain his strength from the weight loss. Consistent with his turbulent state of training, some voice in the camp advised him to eat pancakes to fuel up for the fight. Ravenous, he ate a mountain of them.

Stretching in the locker room of the Summit in Houston, Termite listened to the game plan. "Press him, Termite, bully him, hit him and tie him up." Bill repaired a sparring cut under Termite's eye with frozen Vaseline. Mentally, he was so far away from the fight, the biggest payday of his life, the pinnacle of his career. He needed Potato Pie's voice in his head. Standing at the entrance to the ring, with the wildly cheering crowd, Termite jumped up and down, unfortunately, his stomach moved in a much different pattern. The heap of pancakes shifted and churned. "Oh, God," he thought.

46

The gloves of the two twenty-three year olds had barely touched when Termite charged Davis, hitting him in the ribs and keeping him near the ropes. Termite threw more punches, but Davis's were more effective. Termite head butted and held, tried to make a war of it. Termite hit and held him so Howard could not hit. Howard's incredible speed put him in control by the fifth round. Termite had a devastating eighth round with combinations by Davis opening the cut that bled profusely down Termite's face. By the end of the fight, Termite's sole hope rested in swinging for a knockout. Distressed by the loss, Termite gave Davis all the credit, "Howard Davis is a tremendous fighter." He also revealed his understated view of the bout, "I felt uncomfortable trying to fight a pressing fight. I'm more at ease when I'm moving and boxing."

The following month, *Texas Monthly* magazine ran a feature article entitled, "The Fatal Pancakes." The photograph featured Termite, holding a fork with his boxing gloves on, sitting over a mass of steaming pancakes. The trainers never lived it down.

After the Davis fight, threads in Termite's life unraveled faster than he could repair them. Linda was weary of being Termite's Watkins' wife; the support person in the shadows while he signed autographs and gave interviews. She wanted, after five years, a life of her own. No loss in the ring prepared him for the pain of packed boxes stacked in the living room of their home near Cimarron Elementary, yards from the baseball field where his boxing career started thirteen years ago.

He struggled. An empty house, a blur of trainers, and a nagging feeling that he refused to admit was there. Termite was growing tired of boxing. He was weary of running endless miles at a time of day that the only shop open was the Dunkin Donuts on Uvalde Road. Termite wanted to eat a pack of M&M's without the reminder in every bite of the pain required in working them off. So many sacrifices, and no title – worse, yet, the fun was gone.

Fun soon arrived in an eccentric package. Tony Gardner first saw Termite box as an amateur against Richard Lord when he was a corner man for another fighter. He looked over and saw a kid half the size of the other fighter and said, "Who's that kid boxing the big kid's ears off?" As the manager of the Orlando Sports Stadium, Tony had followed Termite's career and had seen him box many times. At the time of the Davis fight, Pete Ashlock, the millionaire owner of the arena and boxing promoter, asked Tony to go to Houston and "watch over Termite." Mr. Ashlock was a friend of the Watkins and wanted Termite to be in the best shape mentally and physically for the fight. In reality, he wanted Tony to be sure that Termite stayed out of trouble. After a few weeks, Tony called Mr. Ashlock and informed him, "This thing's backwards – the kid needs to watch over *me*. He's a good Christian kid, doesn't cuss, and doesn't party, nothing."

They were the most unlikely team. Tony, a lanky, cowboy hat wearing, former boxer was untamed. Traveling together, Termite tried to change Tony's ways. "Tony, why don't you cut all this womanizing, drinking, stuff out?" Tony always laughed and had the same reply, "Because I don't want to."

Tony did not inspire or motivate, he just made boxing fun again. His loyalty and sense of humor came at the right time. His wit was evident in one of Termite's last matches of his career. Termite came over to the corner, and told Tony that he was seeing two boxers. Knowing Termite would never throw in the towel, Tony said, "Well, son, you'd better hit both of them S.O.B.'s 'cause one of them is kicking your butt."

Termite's corner finally had some semblance of balance again. Henry 'Hank' Grooms was Termite's primary coach, a highly technical trainer with tremendous knowledge, but for a boxer who craved motivation, he was low keyed and professional. Where Potato Pie would incite a riot in Termite's mind before a bout, Henry quietly went over strategies. Tony quickly grew to love Termite and providing the nurturing side of the team; the motivational hole was never replaced.

Every bit of expertise in the corner would be called upon in the bout that Termite had visualized for fourteen years. The world championship fight against Saoul Mamby would take place on October 2, 1980 on a double main event with Muhammad Ali and Larry Holmes, the much touted, "Last Hurrah." Fought in over 100 degrees in the camera lights, it was a match that a true boxing aficionado would appreciate. Mamby was incredibly hard to hit – so was Termite. Both were thinking, technical fighters who used the angles. Feints, jabs, and a high number of body shots were incorporated. So many kidney shots were absorbed by each man that both boxers urinated blood after the fight. It was an incredibly tough fight in which both boxers hurt at the end. The reigning champ, Mamby, got the decision.

The dream was gone, the fire barely a spark. From the first day at Red Shield Gym, he had great certainty that he would be a champion some day. The heartache could be measured in every year, every cut, and every mile. He'd lost the fight of his life; millions in future earnings vanished in the last fifteen rounds of his career. Numb and dazed, his mother Wanda expressed some news that the family had concealed before the fight. In the locker room at Caesar's Palace in Las Vegas, Termite learned that his great life-long buddy, Terry DeWitt, had perished in a car accident. Too stunned for absorption, a subsequent blow followed: his great-grandmother had passed during the week as well. At his most bitter point in the sport he loved, nothing felt real. Termite went back to Texas to mourn, to mend, and to regroup.

The alarm sounded at 4:30, but Termite turned it off. What is an appropriate routine when an entire life's work has crumbled? There would be no running today or any day for the next eighteen months. All of his time had been strictly controlled by his boxing dream since a young age. No more. He wanted to have some fun. His new exercise regimen consisted of country and western dancing until 2:00 A.M. at local clubs. Everything he never did at sixteen or eighteen or twenty-two he did now. He compacted eight years of missed partying into one and a half years. Termite's celebrity boxing status mixed with the club scene brought temptations he'd never

49

known. A stream of women he barely knew, hardly remembered any of their names, entered and exited his out-of-control life.

The crazy life he was living came to an end when he met Sharla McNeese. Beginning as a friendship, she liked Termite for who he was, in fact, she knew little about boxing. A North Shore girl, she had an easy temperament and a loving heart. Her primary concern was being a good mother to her thirteen month old baby, Jared. Termite fell in love with both of them. To be a part of their lives, Termite had to adjust to her calmer lifestyle where the main priority was raising her son. Termite became a father to a son he'd always wanted and a husband to a woman he cherished. Sharla's composed nature balanced Termite's off-the-charts energy level. He was a risk taker who had lived a most unusual life, accustomed to being the center of attention. She was comfortable in a supporting role and took the hoopla around Termite the boxer with the proverbial grain of salt. Settled and happy, it was time to hit the gym.

And he hit the road for another title run. He won his fights, but with pain due to slightly slower reflexes from the long break in training. He'd built his career on hitting and not being hit; now he was getting hit and getting cut. One fight, he was cut five times in early rounds. Bill shot adrenalin in one cut while Tony held another cut closed to keep the ref from stopping the fight. His decision to retire came in a spinning locker room at the Orange Bowl. Nauseous and seeing double, he held a sock filled with ice to the cuts around his eyes. With a clear understanding that he would never retire a champion, the announcement came with only his dad and Thomas Bonk, a sports writer for the *Houston Post*. Adept at winning over the media since an early age, it was not his finest oratory hour. He simply said, "This is not for me. I ain't no fool."

Retirement at twenty-six was a curious thing. Most men don't retire with a toddler and a brand new baby girl, Tessa. Financially, the young Watkins family could survive for a while without employment for Termite – but not for too long. What does a boxer put on a resume for job skills – a wicked left hook? Friends he'd known in high school were now out of college, working in law offices, oil refineries, and classrooms. Not quite sure where to start, he dabbled in everything.

Construction companies, pest control, and a bail bonds company were a few of the industries he tackled. As the old joke goes, "He made two fortunes; unfortunately, he lost three." Houses were lost and cars towed by banks. Not able to pay a storage facility's fee, Termite's Olympic and Golden Gloves jackets disappeared. Pulling up to a red light in a beat-up car that burned two quarts of oil a day, an old North Shore buddy in the next lane yelled to him, "Boy, you've sure gone downhill!"

Downhill couldn't begin to explain what Termite was going through. Sliding farther and farther away from his faith, his family, and his friends, everything Termite treasured was slipping away. On the exterior, it was the same Termite, smiling and trying to please everyone. He coached T-Ball, volunteered at school, and shook hands with former fans. On the inside, he was hurting. A man who had accomplished every goal he'd set for himself from age ten, he simply could not deal with the loss of that title fight. This wasn't how it was supposed to end – scraping for a living, having vehicles repossessed. He was now a down-and-out guy who could not pay his bills, couldn't support his new family. An overachiever his whole life, he was the epitome now of an underachiever. The reality of his new life had a bitter sting, and he could not handle it.

The man who had preached to students across the country the importance of making good choices made one that almost ruined his life. Termite, at age twenty-seven, made a choice to try drugs to relieve the pain of what he saw as his failed life. Cocaine numbed the painful void that was pounding in his head. Everything he'd believed in he abandoned, and the things he didn't believe in, he was doing. A man who used to begin his day in prayer now awoke with the immediate thought of where he could secure the drug and how he would pay for it. Funds sorely needed for his two children were diverted to his drug use. Sharla knew about it and expressed her distaste for this new lifestyle, but Termite persisted. He was so deep into it, he could not stop. Ashamed of his weakness, ashamed of what he'd become, the worse things got the more he needed the drug. Four years passed, and Sharla, always a woman to "Stand by her man," had lost her patience with her husband. Calling him at work, she issued the ultimatum, "Termite, it's your family or the drug, make a choice."

Termite could not lose them, but cocaine had taken over his soul. There was one man who could help him. Johnny Brady. Friends for life, it was Johnny, the preacher's kid, who used to light up cigars with Termite as young kids and play pranks on unsuspecting neighbors while the Watkins held Bible meetings in their home. It was hard to know who influenced whom in their early years, because they were both in trouble so much of the time.

Johnny Brady, now thirty-one like his buddy Termite, had followed a different path than his friend, a path that surprised many of his former classmates. Johnny followed not only Christ's footsteps, but his father's as well into the ministry. In fact, it was Johnny who performed Sharla and Termite's wedding ceremony.

Termite needed him. With their long history, Johnny understood Termite's huge heart, but also his weaknesses. Termite pulled into Woodforest Baptist Church, the same place where the two boys had thrown tiny gum balls in women's hair. Termite was back in his old church, but this time for help. Sitting in Johnny's office, the two men talked for a long while. Johnny was stunned. As close as they were, the young pastor had no hint of Termite's drug use. He still saw Termite as the disciplined boxer who rarely drank even a sip of liquor and adamantly refused to allow drugs in his life. Johnny took Termite's hands, and they prayed for a long time for God to re-take Termite's life. Termite broke down in a tremendous release. He let it go, bawled like a baby, everything came out. He cried about what he'd become and what he had not become. The healing process began, and Termite, a few blocks from his childhood home, rededicated his life to Christ.

This was a new start. He had to overcome what had overcome him. Termite formulated a game plan that was as rigid as his old training regimen. Every minute was accounted for with something positive; there was no time for the negative. Termite mapped out every day to become successful financially and personally, to provide for and keep his family next to him. Trouble was on practically every block, because he knew which school teachers, ex-athletes, and businessmen used cocaine.

He planned every second of every day to keep himself out of trouble. Setting his alarm for 5:00 to emulate his old running time, he awoke, got on his knees and prayed. He prayed for help and guidance, and closed every prayer with, "O.K., Lord, it's in your hands." While the children and Sharla slept, he read the Bible, *studied* the Bible at their kitchen table. He concluded his morning "training" session with motivational reading.

He missed boxing, so he trained boxers. It wasn't the same as being in the ring, but it gave him the opportunity to redeliver all that wealth of boxing knowledge into younger boxers coming up in the sport. He worked, primarily in the family pest control business. He wasn't financially successful, but the family was surviving. Termite took comfort in an unlikely source – Thomas Edison. He'd re-read his biography so many times that he'd practically memorized it. When asked why Edison kept trying to invent the light bulb after so many failures, his response was, "I've discovered 10,000 ways that don't work, which means I'm closer to finding one way that does."

Years began to pile up, and still he could not reconcile in his mind how he'd lost that title fight. In the middle of the night, Sharla frequently found him sobbing at the edge of the bed, reliving that fifteen round nightmare of a fight against Saoul Mamby. The second-guessing made for restlessness; he still felt like a boxer. Termite had a tape of the fight sent by Mike Tyson with a note that said, "Termite, I told you that you won the championship. Here's the living proof." Had he won? The tape of the fight rolled through the screen in his brain night after night. Even when he had some financial success, it just didn't provide the satisfaction, the same importance, of chasing his dream in boxing.

Six years from his retirement dulled the memories of the painful side of boxing: the burst kidney, cracked nose, and cut eyes. A millionaire retail owner in Houston came with a proposition. He'd pay Termite a salary for his comeback. The publicity would benefit his stores and Termite could renew his quest for a world title while providing for his family.

Termite's thirty-three year old body began training. His first day back at the gym, he hadn't anticipated sparring; he just wanted to hit the bags to shake loose. Reggie Johnson, two-time world titleholder, needed a sparring partner. Termite knew he had no business being in the ring, but found himself climbing through the ropes anyway. Pulling on gloves for the first time in several years, they were surprisingly comfortable. They traded pleasantries, touched gloves, and the left-handed Reggie immediately popped Termite right in the nose with his first jab. In sixteen years of boxing, his nose had been cracked probably a dozen times, but it had never been broken. Blood spewed, saturating his shirt, shorts, and gloves in the first ten minutes of his comeback. A trainer at the gym placed his thumbs on each side and popped it back into place. They battled for three rounds toe-to-toe, with coaches and fighters looking on. After the exchange, Reggie joked, "Old man, you still got it!"

He sure felt the "old" part of Reggie's comment. The rigorous training nearly killed him. Termite placed heating pads and Ben Gay on his legs in the morning just so he could get out of bed. The 20,000 miles he'd put on his knees in his first career paled in comparison to the pain the three miles each morning caused now. Of course, the quote he gave for the paper, "I'm in better condition than I ever was when I was younger," was a stretch. A more accurate depiction was that his body could not handle the abuse it once took, and his reflexes were slower. He could see the openings; he just could not react as quickly.

54

Still, he found a way to win; it just wasn't nearly as pretty. He fought in Arizona several times with George Foreman, who was also on the comeback trail. Four knockouts in a row were impressive for a fighter of any age. He hurt and he wanted to go home to Sharla, Jared, and Tessa, but he was undefeated in his first nine fights and focused on another title shot. He missed Little League, and homework time, and the life of a normal dad. His last fight forced the decision. Breaking his right hand in the second round, he continued fighting and knocked the boxer out in round eight with his fractured right. He went back home to Deer Park, Texas for the last time. Sports reporters and boxers had described him as classy, dignified, clever, quick, and even dirty. Whatever the adjective, right now, he just wanted to be called Dad.

In 1990, Termite put his gloves away for the last time, and stored them in the garage next to the blue Rubbermaid bins full of newspaper clippings. Burt Darden of the Houston Chronicle once wrote, "Termite Watkins will do whatever it takes to get the job done." What he had to live with now is that he hadn't gotten the job done - the illusive title - he had so passionately sought.

His family had paid the financial price of a man chasing his dream. Termite was now single-mindedly focused on making their lives more comfortable. Fourteen hour days in the family exterminating business reaped a living, but he didn't want to just get by. Like every other father, he wanted more for this family. He was determined to make their lives better.

Termite called Ralph Herrera, a friend from high school, about getting a job with his employer, a local car dealership. Ralph said, "Termite, they're not hiring, but let me see what I can do." He called back, "Termite, listen, I got you a meeting, but you've got to go in there and show them why they need you." Termite was working so many hours in exterminating that he didn't even have time to change for the interview. He arrived at the sales manager's office with blue work pants, a blue work shirt with "Champion Exterminating" on it, work boots, baseball cap, and a distinct aroma of pesticides.

Termite looked across the desk at a man, impeccably dressed in a business suit, who was ten years younger than Termite. The sales manager was blunt, "Look, we're not hiring and I'm only interviewing you because your friend requested it of me." He came to the point quickly, "Tell me...why *should* I hire you?" It was hard. The proud former contender, sitting in mud-caked work boots fresh from crawling under a house, forced to ask for a job from a kid in a tailored suit. Termite's battered confidence rose in him, "Because if you don't, the best salesman you've ever seen will walk out the door." Obviously perturbed, the interviewer asked, "But you've never even sold a car, what makes you think you're so good at it?" Termite needed this job, a chance to make more money. "I just know that I'll be the best salesman you'll have." The sales manager wasn't quite sure what to make of this ex-boxer in exterminator's gear, but he decided to give him a shot. "Be here at 9:00 Monday morning for a training class." Termite protested, "But I don't have time to take a training class, I'm ready to get going." The sales manager repeated the instructions more emphatically, "Be here at 9:00 for the class."

Termite, accustomed to his early morning ritual, arrived on Monday, but at 8:00, before the sales staff arrived. He saw a customer milling about and struck up a conversation. Honest with the customer that it was his first day, Termite got a key and they took a test drive. Not knowing the business, he had to answer the customer's questions by tracking down answers back and forth around the building. He sold his first car, but he missed the sales meeting.

Tuesday morning, Termite arrived again at 8:00, trying to duplicate his prior day's success. Again, he sold a car before the sales class started. On Wednesday, he sold two. The general manager, known for a bit of a temper, approached Termite. Nervous about getting reprimanded, he blurted out, "I'm sorry for not making it to the classes." She interrupted him with a smile, "Termite, just forget about the sales classes and continue what you're doing." Termite, for the first time in his life, earned six figures that year. The next year, he taught the sales classes that he never attended. He rose to the top of the business, placing in the top percentage of all salesmen in General Motors.

Permanently retired from boxing since 1990, Termite missed the sport he loved terribly, but he felt a great accomplishment in achieving a level of financial success for his family. Sharla and the family were comfortable and settled. They had definitely earned that security so lacking in the early years. By answering God's call to Iraq, Termite brought a different type of instability to the family he so loved. He hated to leave, but he had to answer the call.

5

A World Away

The ten-year-old boy draped his arm over the brown sofa in his dad's office at the Al-Shabab Sports Club in downtown Baghdad. Najah's curious eyes scanned the desk as his dad paid the monthly bills for the club. Every day during the summer months, he accompanied his father, Salah Ali, to work. He studied everything that the former Arab Champion boxer did, because Najah's aspiration in life was certain - to be exactly like his father. When Salah exited the office to oversee activities in the weight room or on the soccer field, Najah quickly sat in the old metal chair, scooted the tired rollers up to the light wood desk and got to work. Pen in hand, he scribbled out pretend checks and answered pretend phone calls about the vast facility. He looked importantly out the window and gazed at the cars entering the front gate of the walled, one-story building. His father's footsteps interrupted his "work" and he jumped back to the couch.

It wasn't just the boxing that Najah wanted to emulate, but his dad's character as well. Warm and compassionate, the 122-pound, 1984 champion was the epitome of a family man and highly supportive of the children's activities. He fully comprehended Najah's dream of being a boxer, but Salah agreed with his wife that academics were the top priority in the Ali family. Najah could train at home with his heavy bag and jump rope, and his father worked regularly with him on stance, rhythm, and technique, but he was not allowed to fight competitively. At 7:00 every evening, the boxers arrived at the gym. Najah absorbed the lessons his father, a former army boxing coach, provided to the boxers, memorizing every piece of advice.

June and July of 1990 was quiet. Every morning, the father and son drove the half-hour drive to downtown Baghdad. Except for Fridays. Fridays in Iraq are for worship, and the family attended mosque. After mosque, Najah, his younger brother, his dad, and uncle headed to the Tigris River for fishing. Standing on the bank of the river, the men cast their lines, equipped with metal weights, hooks, and minnows. They had no rods or reels, or even cane poles, nor did they need them to bring home great catches every week. The boys engaged in their conversations and the men in theirs. The conversations, whether at the river, the gym, or even at home, never included any discussion of Saddam Hussein or politics. Salah had emphasized in the sharpest of tones to his family that, for their safety, they remain silent on anything remotely controversial.

Events in August of 1990 brought tremendous trepidation for the family and other Iraqis as Saddam Hussein ordered the invasion of Kuwait. The subsequent naval blockade by the Americans led Salah to believe that war was imminent. The family home was situated only two miles from the Baghdad airport and a certain target. Bombs were not the father's primary concern, however. Salah had grave worries about Hussein's use of chemical weapons and the possible retaliation by the Americans. The father excluded the children from any discussions of the consequences of any upcoming war, but the children heard the hushed tones of their parents in their small Baghdad home.

Normalcy existed at school for Najah; the bright child with the infectious smile. Segregated by gender, the primary school had well over 2,000 students, with over forty-five teenagers packed into each classroom. The male instructors maintained strict discipline with corporal punishment and a generous amount of yelling for the tiniest of infractions. Any student arriving without homework faced paddling, as did any student who disrupted class. Najah loved learning and rarely faced those academic repercussions – his paddling came from moving around too much. When time came to head for the soccer field for recess, Najah sped down the halls adorned with pictures of Hussein. His pent up energy had to be released, despite instructors' warnings to walk.

In mid-January of 1991, Najah returned home to find his parents packing their belongings. The escalation of tension between Iraq and the newly formed Coalition forces were at the point that Salah felt adamant about a temporary relocation. They drove seven hours north to a small village in the mountains of Iraq. The tiny farmhouse belonged to Najah's cousin and was already inundated by other family members who had fled Baghdad. While Operation Desert Storm commenced on January 17, Najah played in the countryside of northern Iraq. Salah and the other men listened intently to news reports, and when the fighting stopped, they returned home. Najah had heard from people outside his family that Americans were evil, and the boy broached the topic with his father. "Son," he told him, "Don't make a decision about people until you meet them yourself, then decide what you think."

Najah continued to train in his small garage and in the summers returned to work with his father. Even at the gym, their faith was paramount. The call to prayer came five times a day, and the men in the gym dutifully unrolled their mats and prayed. Older men often had thick, discolored calluses on their foreheads from their heads resting on the floor repeatedly for prayer.

At night, he watched videos of his father's fights and dreamed of having the glorious career his father had enjoyed. Najah's mother, Amera, remained resolute about her son's academics. In addition to opening career doors, being in a university would allow Najah to minimize his mandatory military time. Salah had done his compulsory military duty, but as a boxing coach, thus avoiding the front lines in the prolonged war with Iran. All boys who did not attend a university served in the military for three years – those exiting after college only served half of that time. Minimizing their son's active duty was paramount. Iraq had been engulfed in so many military endeavors over the past twenty years that the adult male population had dwindled to 40% of its inhabitants.

When Najah reached sixteen, the aspirations of their son could no longer be avoided. Father and son convinced Amera that Najah could keep his grades up while boxing, and his competitive training commenced. Once in, his mother became as big of a supporter as his father and trainer. Najah's arrivals home with bloodied noses and black eyes were met with, "You look just like your father did."

Najah rose through the ranks of Iraq's boxing elite, defeating Saraka, one of the country's best. He won the Arab games twice, the same competition his father had dominated. His quickness was remarkable, and he punched like a big man; however those traits failed to define the boxer's real strength – he had heart. The sweetest guy in the world outside of the ring, his determination to win in the ring was incomparable. Najah hit the ceiling of boxing in the region; there was no place left to go – no pros, no Olympics. He'd beaten every opponent in his weight class in the country.

It was time to keep his promise to his mom. He started his academic career in a university in Baghdad, majoring in computer science. Najah continued to train, however, just for the love of sport. Always bright and inquisitive about everything, he excelled in school. One class, however, gave him difficulty – English. He received the first failing grade of his life and, being a competitor in school as well as boxing, was furious with himself. That "F" caused Najah to repeat English, thus extending his university life one extra session. It was the most fortunate failing of his young life. His last semester, war was on the horizon with America again. Being a university student, he was exempted from military service.

In the spring of 2003, the ultimatum laid down by President Bush passed without acquiescence by Hussein, and Baghdad again braced itself. A few evenings later, bombs landed all around the family home near the Baghdad airport. Aunts, cousins, and siblings ran screaming to the back room. Najah pulled a mattress off the closest bed and pressed it to the front windows to deflect the flying glass. His father comforted the family and grabbed another mattress to assist his son. That night, Najah counted over forty bombs as he shielded the family from glass. When the bombings receded the next morning, Najah and his father moved the family to the outskirts of Baghdad, far away from the airport, where they settled into a tiny rental home. The old man they rented from refused to take any money from the family. Najah and his dad hooked a generator for the family and listened to broadcasts on the war. Water had to be secured a mile away from the house, a chore Najah handled several times a day.

   After a week, Salah felt it was safe enough to return home and begin repairs on their lifelong home. A rough time to be a new college graduate on the job market, Najah took the only job he could find in a furniture factory; his dad began a construction job generated by the reconstruction effort. Six days a week, Najah boxed. He had to walk around bombed craters and stepped over rubble in the road to get to the gym, but he boxed. He walked around coalition soldiers in tanks to get to the gym, but he persisted in his training. When asked later if he worried about walking around Baghdad amidst the danger, he responded, "This is my country; I will always go where I want in my own country."

6

One Chance in a Million

The buzz of the alarm clock at 4:45 A.M. met with a quick reaction. Termite did not want to wake the other KBR men in the huge tent positioned behind the former Babel Hotel in Hilla, Iraq. The men worked until at least eleven each night seven days a week and sleep was a precious commodity. Clutching his flashlight, he stepped outside and gave his teeth a quick brush, rinsed with bottled water, and spat into the sand. With his flashlight aimed on the path, he watched for obvious dangers like vipers, but his mind was more occupied with items such as bags or cans – anything that could contain explosives. Arriving at the back patio of the hotel, now the CPA headquarters, he walked up the eight steps to his new makeshift boxing facility.

The flaming wreck outside of Hilla in the Suburban left Termite with virtually no clothing for a while – even the pictures of his family were charred. Purchased from a street vendor at the gate compound, he had two choices in his wardrobe: lime green tropical shorts or hot pink flowery shorts. He was partial to the hot pink, and endured the comments. "Hey, Termite, you're looking awfully pretty today," one of the Aussie soldiers teased. Termite always laughed and said, "Thanks, I do feel mighty cute." In a sea of camouflage, Termite was a rose bush. Only a former contender could have the confidence in his manhood to dress like a vendor hawking beach umbrellas in the middle of military men in a war zone.

Termite's beginning boxing class arrived first. Stretching and shadow boxing with them, he went over basic techniques in boxing. His students were a mixture of volunteer workers, KBR, and military. Secured from Kuwait, Termite had a speed bag, a heavy bag, jump ropes, and a rowing machine that he'd developed into a circuit-training program. Where the concrete joined together on the back porch was a perfect line for his students to practice the same line drills he'd learned from Kenny Weldon thirty-five years ago. Colonel Bruce arrived with the more advanced classes that centered on developing punches. He had gotten the boxing bug in Umm Qasr with Termite and had expedited the equipment, welders, and everything else to get a program started here in Hilla. Termite trained his men and women. Workers, soldiers, and volunteers gathered at an ungodly hour in immense heat in a fortified compound to learn to box. Termite's tireless optimism replenished their morale for the day's work.

Heading back to the tent at 7:30 to cleanup for his day job, he splashed his face and underarms with a small amount of non-potable water, shaved, and headed to the front gate to meet his Iraqi workers. For three months, he'd only seen the inside of the walled-in compound, comprised of roughly three acres and the three-story building.

A fortress guarded by Gurkhas, the elite special operations forces from Nepal, layers of security were immensely taut. A machine-gun laden Humvee first greeted visitors, followed by an iron gate secured by a Gurkha, then two subsequent guard stations. Winding through those layers, arrivals could see two more Gurkhas with machine guns positioned on the roof of the building twenty-four hours of the day. Highly skilled in martial arts, their traditional weaponry was embellished by their Kukri knives, lethally sharp curved weapons tucked in their webb belts. Any potential infiltrator ran the very real risk of losing his head.

The Iraqi men, some in traditional garb and some in western style clothing, filed through the gate after getting padded down for weapons. Termite greeted his Iraqi friends with kisses on each cheek, an Iraqi custom that he wholly embraced. Initially, all of the Iraqi workers were utilized to clean the former hotel, which had been ransacked by the Iraqi army after Saddam's disappearance early in the war. Room by room, the men worked side by side with Termite as he taught them how to scrub toilets and floors, pull up carpet, whatever needed to be done. Keenly curious about American culture, the Iraqis thirsted for real information about America, and Termite supplied details about choices, freedoms, and culture in America. Ideas about politics (they liked President Bush), to jobs, to religion, to women (why do you give them so much power?) to money were exchanged. Cumbersome at times with their broken English, what mattered most to the Iraqis was that they were being treated with such dignity and respect by their new mentor.

A genuine fondness grew between Termite and the burgeoning ranks of workers. Their affectionate nature took some getting used to for the Texan. At times, he would be walking through the compound and an Iraqi worker would just grab his hand and hold it, much like two little girls walking down the street in Houston. At other times, in appreciation for some small favor he'd rendered, a worker would kiss him repeatedly back and forth on his cheeks. American men were raised to be so detached emotionally; this was such a change in attitude. However, he liked the emotional nature of the Iraqi men. In fact, he developed a love for the Iraqi people and found himself becoming more expressive in their midst.

The dialogue between Termite and the workers led to changes in job titles. While pulling out carpet in a room, two of the workers kept saying to him, "Automobiles?" Termite just nodded. Scrubbing floors, the question continued, "Automobiles?" He finally took the guys to Randolf, the chief mechanic who kept all the KBR and CPA vehicles running. "Look," Termite said, "I don't know if they know anything about cars, but they sure keep talking about the automobiles. See if you can use them." A few hours later, Randolf came back, "Termite, these guys are incredible. They can do anything to a 2003 Suburban without a manual or anything, they can do it all." The next time Termite saw the new Iraqi mechanics, they each kissed him eight or ten times on each cheek in gratitude, "Thank you, thank you, Mr. Termite."

He was a one-man employment agency. Those with electrical experience he routed to one place, carpentry, another. One worker, dubbed "Little Termite" learned everything he could about pest control, following Termite around to set rodent baits. Those with undetermined skills he kept on as cleaners. One morning, one of the Gurkhas called the main building and said, "Tell Termite he has some guests at the gate." Iraqi men he'd never seen before greeted him saying, "Mr. Termite, I work for you." Word traveled fast in neighboring villages that a man named Termite might be able to help them. What he really did was just listen and help. Termite just loved helping them.

Two of the Iraqi workers he enjoyed the most were Maytham and Wayhee, young men in their 20's who worked at the Babel Hotel before the war. Best friends, they worked alongside Termite everyday. Wayhee was married with two girls; Maytham was still single. During one of their many lunchtime conversations, Termite asked, "Why aren't you married, Maytham?" "I will be in five years," he said meekly. "Why five years?" Termite queried. "That's how long it will take me to save enough money for her dowry." Maytham's intended was an old childhood friend who attended a university in Baghdad about one hour north of Hilla. He explained to Termite that he spent much of his time building on a room to his family's home for his future bride, something he was expected to do. "How much money do you need?" Termite asked. Maytham quoted a figure in dinars, which equated to around $500.00 U.S. dollars.

Working with Maytham everyday, Termite's view of his character continued to impress him, and the thought of his friend not being able to afford his wife until he was at least thirty-two bothered Termite. After some reflection and a phone call home to his own wife, Termite gave Maytham the money. Two months later when the bride arrived in Hilla, the consensus of the new couple was that the firstborn child, male or female, would be named Termite, or, in Arabic, "Artha."

What struck Termite about Maytham's quiet friend, Wayhee, was his loving nature and incredible work ethic.

Wayhee scrubbed and cleaned the rooms of the hotel relentlessly, rarely taking a break. Termite supervised several crews throughout the building at this point, and would get dozens of workers started before settling in to work on whatever project Maytham and Wayhee were on. Wayhee did everything he could to stop Termite from working. If Termite picked up a mop, Wayhee would try to take the mop, "No, Mr. Termite, I do it." If Termite started picking up trash, Wayhee would rush over and say, "I do it." Finally, Termite pulled Mayhee and Maytham aside and explained, "Look, I appreciate you not wanting me to work, but I'm here to work *with* you, helping you, but, understand, you do *not* work for me." That concept, in a community raised in fear of the Hussein regime, of authority in general, took a while to absorb. Termite dipped his brush in the bucket and scrubbed the walls. His co-workers joined in.

Short reprieves from work were spent on the rooftop looking over the countryside of Iraq. From that vantage point, he saw far beyond his fenced in yard into the communities of Iraq. Behind the date tree strewn compound was farmland with rows and rows of crops tended by women humped over in their black robes and head coverings. In the immense Iraqi sun, they labored all day with children in tow. The fields emptied for a couple of hours in midday, probably to cook for the men, he reasoned. The lives of Iraqi women in this part of country were so incredibly harsh. The Hilla River flowed near them and Iraqi men in white robes fished from their canoes; downstream, Iraqis bathed in the river. From a different angle, the ancient city of Babylon could be seen. Inside the concrete-bricked walls of the Coalition compound was the West, with televisions and computers; outside, life styles existed much like it did a century ago in this part of Iraq.

Every climb up the stairs to the rooftop deepened Termite's respect for the Gurkhas, quietly seated with their machine guns, eyes peeled around the perimeter of the camp. Deployed with the British on most every conflict, their intense loyalty combined with deadly skills and courage allowed

68

employees to sleep at night knowing the Ghurkas were just above their bedroom ceilings. Termite and the soldiers talked about the beauty of the green irrigated fields surrounding them. Other days, Termite asked about Nepal and their families back home. The Gurkhas' favorite topic was boxing, and they questioned him about his experiences and techniques. Every day, this boy from North Shore learned more about the world in that small compound than he ever thought possible.

One day, Colonel Bruce pulled Termite aside from his crew and said, "Come with me. You've been invited by the Gurkhas to attend a special ceremony tonight." Termite and the Colonel walked the 200 yards over to the roundhouse, a building Saddam Hussein once used as a disco. Behind the building was a simmering fire built hours ago by the Gurkhas.

Termite joined General Walters, Mike Gfoeller, the second in charge of the coalition in southern Iraq, and Colonel Bruce in a circle with the Gurkhas. In the middle of the circle was a reddish brown goat, with a rope tied high on its neck, with very nervous eyes. General Buck and Mike both spoke about their genuine appreciation for the bravery and dedication the Gurkhas had shown on this assignment and their illustrious history in Nepal and Great Britain. A Gurkha explained quietly to the assembled group the significance of the decapitation of the goat. If the head fell in one clean slice of the Kukri knife, the upcoming year would be a success; the opposite would be true if the task required more than one slice. A soldier held grass in front of the goat's mouth coaxing it to stretch its neck out over a small board under the neck. The Gurkha lifted the razor sharp knife over his head, and sliced right through the goat's neck, which fell in one piece to the ground. The other Gurkhas quickly slung the goat's body down until the twitching of the animal's nerves ceased. After bleeding the goat into a bucket, various organs were extracted and cooked in a sauce from the blood. The Americans and British went back to their work for a few hours while the goat meat cooked on the fire. They returned to eat the meat, cut into small pieces on toothpicks. The Gurkhas graciously thanked the visitors for

69

participating in their centuries old custom. They all needed a good year.

Another month passed in Hilla. Employees celebrated birthdays in the dining hall and made whispered calls home to their wives late at night. Seven-day workweeks of eighteen-hour days erased the seams of the calendar. General Walters returned to Texas and Mike Gfoeller became the administrator of the coalition in southern Iraq. Still in a tent, it was now a tent with plywood walls so that each worker had a separate cubicle. Termite's pest control assignments forced him to travel across southern Iraq, disappointing his boxing students and his Iraqi friends in Hilla. Colonel Bruce told him, "Morale really suffers when you're not here." Hilla had become home, and he missed it when he traveled.

The CPA needed to expand its borders around the building to add portable living containers and extra security. Those expansion needs encroached on a local villager's land, and he was understandably angry about the situation. Colonel Bruce asked Termite to accompany him to the neighboring sheik's home a couple of miles from their building to discuss the situation. The sheik of the Jezra tribe was a thin, one-eyed gentleman in his seventies. A leader responsible for four or five hundred members, many in the sheik's village were workers that Termite knew quite well.

Leaving the compound in three Suburbans with two or three shooters per vehicle, the lead vehicle shot out onto the blacktop road to cut off any traffic then caught up and resumed the lead. The trio of black vehicles flew past the drive-in theater built entirely for one patron, Saddam Hussein. Consisting of a large screen and a tall, concrete-blocked fence, the dictator and his entourage generally watched *The Godfather*, Hussein's favorite movie. They also passed a wide range of domiciles, from one-room adobe huts with only five-foot ceilings to more comfortable homes. Most of the homes had been added on repeatedly, as sons brought home wives and needed their own space. Almost all had tall walls around the perimeter for protection.

Only a few minutes away, they turned into a dirt road that led to a cul-de-sac. Word had spread so quickly that they were coming, that, by the time they reached their destination, scores of children followed the vehicles. Positioning the vehicles for a quick emergency exit, the shooters remained by the cars during the entire business meeting, equipped with machine guns and two- way radios.

Sheik Humsey and about thirty Iraqi men greeted them with kisses and escorted them into a long room. Seated on chairs, couches, and cross-legged on the floor, the men exchanged pleasantries while they drank Chi tea, a mixture of strong hot tea and sugar served in a small shot style glass. No women were visible, but more than fifty Iraqi children crowded around the window, fascinated by the proceedings.

Termite and Colonel Bruce, dressed in Dockers and polo style shirts, sat across from the gray whiskered Sheik Humsey in his traditional gown. Through a translator, negotiations began. The sheik, concerned like any astute politician about his constituents' needs, talked about the long distance the village children walked to school, about the dirt road that always flooded in the rain, and about the one water pump that supplied the entire village. Colonel Bruce explained the coalition's need to enlarge the perimeter of the compound. The sheik encouraged Colonel Bruce and Termite to hire more Jezra workers. Colonel Bruce countered about security issues with one bellicose villager adjacent to coalition property. After the give and take of business concluded, the Iraqi men stretched out a long blue plastic tarp on the floor for the food. The men brought the dishes in, carp and goat, rice, custard, and goat's milk. The entire delegation sat cross-legged on the floor around the tarp. Sheik Humsey, seated in the center facing the guests, reached in with his right hand for a piece of carp, signaling the others to begin. Light dinner conversation circled about the table – fishing, the children at the window, the sheik's home. Just a normal dinner amongst a Texas exterminator, a British colonel, and a village chief, with three armed shooters twenty feet from the front door.

71

After dinner, Termite and Colonel Bruce exchanged kisses with all of the men, a somewhat time-consuming process considering the numbers, and agreed to continue the dialogue on areas of concern. At one point, a gunshot rang out from the neighborhood. The sheik calmed them saying, "Don't worry, you're safe here."

Subsequent meetings provided Termite with a political education few could attain at any Ivy League school. The issues that mattered here in southern Iraq: quality education, decent roads, and jobs were the same as citizens rallied for in the States. Gatherings were arranged through one of the sheik's nephews, who ran a crew at the compound. "Termite, my uncle wants you to come by soon." Termite would reply, "Tell the sheik I'll be by on Thursday night."

Trust between the two groups became so solid that the villagers guarded the Chevy Suburbans during the meetings. Concerns were communicated; common ground reached. The sheik offered protection and security intelligence for the coalition. The coalition members wanted to get them their school. Initiating a corruption-free bidding process similar to the states, an Iraqi contractor began the work. Colonel Bruce was redeployed prior to the school's completion and told Termite, "Get that school built for those kids." Not only did they get their school, named "The Liberation School," but the dirt road leading to the school was also blacktopped so the children wouldn't have to walk through the mud. The coalition expanded its perimeters, adding new portable living containers and an additional security layer. Threats ceased from the Jezra neighbor who gave up land unwillingly to the coalition. The last job finished was the electric water pump, drastically enhancing the Iraqis' lives. It was an example of what could happen in Iraq when mutual respect and open minds met in a living room off a dirt road in Hilla.

But scores of smaller things happened as well. KBR and coalition workers pooled their resources for a wheel chair shipped from the states for the ten-year-old daughter of one of their newfound Iraqi automobile mechanics. Bedridden her

72

entire life, the only time the little girl left her home was in her dad's arms. A crying father whose previous English vocabulary was limited to "automobile" learned "thank you" as the men delivered it to the home.

When kidney stones rendered Wayhee in extreme pain, Termite paid for the doctor - Wayhee counted out his change. One of the older workers had prostate problems like Termite; he gave him his entire supply of Saw Palmetto to relieve the symptoms. They were in a place where so much help was needed. In Hilla, KBR employees and coalition staff members had all signed on for the job due to some idealistic hope that they could make a difference in the world. They did.

Termite's ability to get the job, any job, done resulted in a job offer from CPA to run construction projects in the area for the coalition. His purpose at KBR was to support the coalition; now he was part of the coalition staff and received support from KBR. This also meant that, after six months in a tent in Iraq, he got his own room at the compound. In his enhanced role, Termite's relationship with Mr. Mike Gfoeller, the civilian administrator over the southern region of Iraq, tightened.

Mr. Gfoeller inspired Termite. A champion of building democracy in the region, Mr. Gfoeller understood the Arab viewpoint from other positions he had held in Saudi Arabia and Bahrain. Fluent in Arabic, "Mr. Mike" as he was often called by the Iraqis, spoke not only their language, but he had a deep appreciation for the ancient culture of the Iraqis. The forty-six year-old's vision was one of tremendous hope and possibilities for his region. As the civilian administrator over six governorates in Southern Iraq, he initiated projects in Hilla, Karbala and Najaf – projects that showed local Iraqis the good things the coalition could do with Iraqi support. Termite's job was to oversee many of these projects, as many as eighteen at a time. Soccer fields, clinics, schools, and youth centers were repaired and built, and telecommunications systems constructed.

Mr. Gfoeller, due to his great ability to communicate the greatness of democracy to the Iraqi people, impacted them in a way that no building project could. He organized democracy training in area centers. The forums discussed rights and responsibilities, free speech, choices, and the importance of voting. After participating in one of the forums, one Iraqi woman said, "It is important to hear others' opinions." "Mr. Mike" was the Thomas Jefferson of south central Iraq. Termite, who spoke only Texan, and Mike, who spoke six languages, both communicated to the Iraqis the same message: we're here to help you change your country.

In addition to overseeing projects under Mr. Gfoeller's supervision, Termite was now an Advisor to the Ministry of Youth Sports in southern Iraq. While in Baghdad securing his new CPA badge for his job with Mr. Gfoeller, Termite stopped by the Ministry of Youth Sports office and offered his services. Upon hearing of his boxing background, they welcomed him as an additional tool in rebuilding the youth sports program in Iraq. Separate from the Olympic Committee, the ministry focused at the grass roots level – building or repairing sports facilities and promoting athletics. In essence, he worked on building projects for the southern region of Iraq and aided in sports issues in that same area.

On a September 2003 morning at the Hilla compound, Termite proceeded through the breakfast line and sat down with his tray and coffee. Mr. Gfoeller walked up to his table, "Mind if I join you, Termite?" Termite felt honored to have one-on-one time with the man he considered the greatest leader he had ever met. Mr. Gfoeller stared pensively at his food; something vitally important weighed on his mind. When he looked up from his food, his determined eyes locked onto Termite's.

"Termite," Mr. Gfoeller chose his words carefully, "What are the chances of getting an Iraqi boxing team ready and someone qualified for the 2004 Olympics in Athens?" Termite's response was swift and certain. Chuckling, he laid out the odds, "Slim to none, maybe one chance in a million." Mr. Gfoeller replied immediately and with tremendous enthusiasm, "Great! We just need that one chance; we don't need the million." A rush of shocked excitement went through

74

Termite's veins. "We'll need money, quite a bit of it, and a facility," Termite started. Mr. Gfoeller explained, "Money seized from Saddam Hussein can fund it, Termite. Anything you need, you let me know. You're in charge of this now. Do whatever it takes." Mr. Gfoeller paused, looked Termite square in the eyes, and left him with this thought, "You're the one who can do this. I *expect* you to get it done." He left a stunned ex-boxer at the breakfast table.

A man who never fulfilled his dream of getting an Olympic medal or a world title now had the chance to instill that dream to a new group of boxers and to provide hope to athletes and a nation. A country so desperate for some good news would soon have a team worthy of their respect. He would make it happen. The newly crowned Iraqi Olympic boxing coach flipped open his yellow legal pad and got busy.

He felt a surge of adrenalin; it was the adrenalin of a boxer readying for the ring – he'd missed that feeling. Late in the night at the compound, Termite felt an urgent need to spread this incredible news. Logging onto Classmates.com for the first time, he scrolled through the North Shore listings until he came upon the name of an old dear friend that he'd lost touch with years ago. "Suzy," he typed, "You'll never believe what just happened. I just became the Olympic boxing coach for the country of Iraq." After filling in the astounding details of the past months, he pressed enter and sent the message onto the girl he'd known even as a toddler.

An Iraqi coach with sandy hair, light eyes, and a drawl was an oddity, and a thorny security issue. As the growing insurgency and subsequent violence against Americans grew around Baghdad, he drove in to meet the assembled boxers. He'd phoned the Iraqi Boxing Federation's president in Baghdad two days earlier, and told him, "I'd like to help you put together an Iraq Olympic boxing team." Requesting the two best boxers in Iraq for each eleven weight divisions, he traveled into Baghdad amid tight security to meet them.

Less than three months after the death of Uday Hussein, Termite's cognizance of Iraq's atrocious recent Olympic history weighed on his mind. Uday, a known murderer and openly called a "psychopath" by one world leader, used his position as the head of Iraq's Olympic Committee to abuse and torture athletes. The soccer players endured the most horrific treatment, including caning – called falaka – on their feet. In the soccer complex a spiked torture device known as an iron maiden sat adjacent to Uday's office; the spikes were worn from use. Even a soccer official who refused to cheat for a team was beaten three times a day with hoses and canes and forced to lie in sewage. Uday had also reportedly beaten a boxer who failed to win in a competition, then exiled him to a cell where he was never seen again.

Termite Watkins, a man who had always fought out of love of the sport, had to win their trust. He could not focus on differences – language, nationalities, religion. Their new coach would concentrate on what they had in common – love of boxing and love of country.

Pulling into the soccer stadium, twenty-four Iraqi men, many barefooted and shirtless, sat on the curb. The Chevy Suburbans zipped around the parking lot. Coming to a halt, the shooters exited first, surveyed the situation, and opened the door for Termite. Only two days after Mr. Gfoeller had told Termite he expected him to get the job done, he was prepared to meet his boxers. Several coaches walked across the parking lot, extending their hands to Termite. With machine-gun armed shooters on each side of him, the coaches escorted him up several flights of stairs to see their boxing facility.

Dusty and dark, the equipment was sparse and worn. The ring, about ½ of the regulation size, was bordered by uncovered hemp rope; the ring floor was wooden and had a hole in it. A few heavy bags hung from the ceiling, but there were no speed or crazy bags, no jump rope platforms, and no hand pads. "Let us show you what we have," the coaches said, motioning to the stairs.

Exiting to the ground floor, the twenty-four men jumped up from the curb, and pulled ripped gloves from their gym bags. These were not sparring gloves, but smaller, ten ounce fighting gloves. Not one fighter had a mouthpiece, headgear, or groin protection. Walking onto the soccer field, one of the coaches spoke a few words in Arabic, and then yelled. "Daum!"

Forty-eight fists flew in an all-out brawl. Half of them boxed shoeless, most with ripped gloves. Hungry fighters eager for an opportunity slammed fists into each other. Within seconds, eyes were cut and noses were bleeding. Termite screamed, "Stop! Stop!" He moved closer to the Iraqi coaching staff. "What are you doing?" he demanded. "Ya'll can't do this! They don't have even have mouthpieces or headgear!" he exclaimed. Pausing for an explanation, one of the coaches finally offered, "That's how we do it."

Every ounce of resolve he summoned to conceal the shock of the reality he had just witnessed. He immediately felt for them. Twenty four men, some in their thirties, trying so hard to impress him – fighting under conditions no boxer in the West would tolerate. What they didn't have struck him, and a place in his heart opened for his new team. Termite smiled his big smile and nodded, thanking the men. To the coaches, he said, "Have them on the bus ready to go back with me to Hilla tomorrow at 10:00 A.M." The coaches nodded in agreement.

Walking towards his vehicle, one of the smallest boxers stopped Termite, and in fairly fluent English, said, "I will go to the Olympics with you, and I will win." Termite remembered him, and praised him, "You've got fast hands." Najah smiled and went back to the team. After the exhibit, a reporter from an Arabic station asked him simply, "What do you think?" Termite exclaimed with passion, "The Iraqi boxers have a lot of heart!" Trying to put a positive face on the boxing disaster he'd just witnessed, he continued, "We're going to do our best to make this happen for the country, and we need the support and help of the Iraqi people." He closed the interview with a slogan he'd made up on the spot. "We are going to show the world that," he paused and raised his fist, "IRAQ IS BACK!"

Termite and his team did not have a minute, a second to waste. Other countries had been training for years –*he* had fifty-seven days until the Olympic trials. Tomorrow morning, he would head back to Hilla with his new team.

It was a new day in Iraqi sports. Without Saddam Hussein or his son, athletes could box, or wrestle, or be a goalie on a soccer field without fear of retribution. Iraq only had one Olympic medal in their entire history. In 1960, a weightlifter secured a bronze for the country. Termite felt so privileged to be the man to make it happen. The pages of his legal pad were curled from use. Equipment needs, costs, training, sparring, coaches, Termite's "to do" lists filled the sheets. As he pulled into the soccer complex, his entire focus was gathering his "boys" and getting to the gym in Hilla.

Concern immediately swept over his face. Where was the bus for the fighters? The coaches present yesterday greeted him in Arabic again, but with a different demeanor. They ushered Termite and his two shooters into a room filled with about twenty-five men, most of whom were Olympic members from the Hussein regime. One shooter remained by the door of the room, alternating his visual scanning between the hallway and the room with the strangers. Termite stood next to a desk at the front of the room, with the other shooter only three feet to his left. A nervous edginess filled the room.

"Where are the boxers?" asked Termite in a civil, but firm tone. The translator repeated the question in Arabic. No answer came, just a buzzing in Arabic resulting from numerous whispered conversations. Termite slammed his hand down on the desk. "Where are the boxers?" he demanded, his temper rising. "Tell me where they are or I'm walking out of here!" The nervous translator relayed the question. To his left, he was aware that the machine gun's tip had changed from the floor to the crowd. His shooter whispered to Termite, "Do you know what you're doing?" Termite responded, "Look, if I don't show who's in charge of this thing right now, it's all over for those boxers."

Finally, Saeed, the Iraqi Boxing Federation president responded. "It's Ramadan, and the fighters are fasting. We would like to discuss with you..." Termite cut him off mid-sentence. "I don't care about Ramadan. You gave your word that the boxers would be here. We've risked our lives coming into Baghdad for these fighters. You'd better have those boxers in Hilla at 10:00 tomorrow morning. If they're even one minute late, just turn the bus around and leave. I'll put this boxing team together with or without your help. If I have to, I'll get my fighters off the streets of Baghdad." The translator's eyes widened nervously, but he repeated the warning. Termite left the building sandwiched between two machine guns and returned to Hilla. It would be tough telling Mr. Gfoeller that he had no boxers.

The next morning, Termite called the Hilla Sports Club to give the manager a "heads-up" about his arrival. Termite's face on Arabic news heightened security awareness around him. The mandatory three Chevy Suburbans backed into the blue gym. The wrought iron gate of the walled facility opened. The driver backed the vehicle to three feet of the front door. After securing the gate, Termite opened his car door and stood in front of the building. His watch read 9:30. They waited. At 9:58, the small white bus arrived from Baghdad.

Termite stood at the door of the bus and greeted each player individually with kisses. The translator stood beside him, providing introductions. He met Zuhair, a 165 pounder who bore a strong resemblance to Sugar Ray Leonard. Saeed's son, Emad, greeted Termite with a huge smile. An Iraq champion heavy weight, Muhammad Galeb, greeted Termite with no expression. Later, Termite discovered the thirty-four-year-old boxer bore scars on his back from Uday's beatings. A 51K fighter, Majeed, exited the bus, also expressionless. Termite smiled and put every ounce of his goodness into each greeting. These were his boys now and they would be treated like Olympians.

Termite led the boxers into the gym and assembled them on the floor for their first meeting. He'd requested two from each weight class, but one boxer in particular was missing – the relentless, quick-handed kid who stopped him on the soccer field.

Termite looked at their faces. They'd packed their bags and left their homes for this opportunity to represent their country at the Olympics. One said to him, "We just want to see our Iraqi flag at the Olympic Games." He had no prepared remarks, no magic words, so he just spoke from his huge boxer's heart:

"You have been held back for so long under Saddam Hussein's reign. You deserve this opportunity. This is your time; you are free now. Freedom means you have a choice. I'm here by choice. I came to Iraq by choice. This is a chance to represent your country, to go down in history as the first boxing team of the new government. You will be the men that your country looks up to. Iraq is now a land of opportunity. We've got a long way to go to get to the Olympics, and a lot of hard work to do." He glanced at Muhammad. "You're safe here, you'll be protected. This is a place where you can box for the love of the sport, not out of fear."

Termite clapped his hands in a rhythm and chanted. "Iraq...is back. Iraq is back. Iraq.....is back, Iraq is back!" He circled the team, clapping and chanting, encouraging the boxers to join him. They clapped, first with tepid enthusiasm, then with greater volume. Termite danced around the team, chanting, "Iraq...is back. Iraq is back!" He pulled one boxer up with him, who danced along chanting. They pulled another boxer, then an Iraqi coach who accompanied the team. The translator danced and chanted. Finally, everyone danced and chanted, some with great gusto, some looking at the exit doors. The walls reverberated with the chant. They had never been to a practice like this. Every team workout from that moment started and ended with the chant.

Two days later, the doors of the Hilla Sports Club opened during their workout, which was being covered by CNN. Najah Ali, the determined young man from the soccer field, walked up to Termite and said simply, "I'm here to be on the team." He had been denied entry on the bus in Baghdad by the boxing federation, and he'd paid his own way to Hilla. After his first workout, the CNN reporter pulled him aside for an interview. His incredibly bright smile warmed the airwaves as he spoke eloquently about this great opportunity being presented to these boxers. Termite grinned at the reporter, "And he can fight!"

7

Fifty-Seven Days, Insha'Allah

The old car backed up to the front door of the Hilla Sports Club, the official training center for the new Olympic team. Two rooftop Iraqi police officers, fresh from coalition training, waved them on with their AK-47's. Dressed in long dresses, their arms, shoulders, and heads covered, the Iraqi women carried the boxes of food into the gym. Quietly, they arranged the lunch offering on foldout tables, setting the paper plates to the side. Steam from the heaping mounds of rice drifted over the chicken and piles of unleavened bread. The Iraqi Olympic boxing team advanced through the line, ladling a chicken-vegetable soup called morgah onto the rice. They each thanked the women from the Fatima Al-Zahra Women's Center and settled into their makeshift card table dining room in the gym. For security reasons, the boxers were prohibited from leaving the facility, day or night. Even though most Iraqis were warm, good people, there was a highly dangerous population of those who opposed coalition presence and anyone who collaborated with them. With the exception of the short walk to the basketball gym for roadwork, their lives existed inside these walls. Consequently, Termite's first priority was getting them fed.

The catering contract was the first for the women's center, located a few miles from the sports facility. But, then again, the women's center was a first for the entire country of Iraq. It took a petite "ball of dynamite," as one lieutenant colonel described her, to found the center. Openly passionate about freedom and human rights, Fern Holland, a young Oklahoma lawyer, worked tirelessly developing the center that would empower Iraqi women. The catering business was just one of their ventures to lift women out of their position as third-class citizens. Iraqi women crowded around the computer center learning new skills, and a lecture hall brought top ranking policy makers to the women of Hilla. Termite's boys needed food, and Fern's women needed work – the match resulted in a new female-owned business landing their first customer.

Western Olympic athletes have access to nutritionists, sports psychologists, and sports therapists; the Iraqi athletes needed shoes and socks. Termite sent Alaa, a vendor known for locating merchandise throughout Iraq, with a wad of cash. Alaa found channels, some probably not entirely legal, to outfit the team. After all, there were no sporting goods chains in Iraq. Fifty-seven days until the first Olympic trials in the Philippines, and some of Iraq's boxers were running sprints with bare feet. The one shabby ring at the facility was a weatherworn fixer upper that had been kept outdoors. The team dragged it indoors, covered the wooden, splintered floor with padding and secured strips of sheets around the ropes. It wasn't pretty, but it was usable.

While Saddam Hussein was on the run, some of his money was being circulated on jump ropes, hand pads, speed bags, and blankets. Bunk beds for twenty-four boxers were squeezed into a vacant room in the facility. More beds were assembled in a room for the three Iraqi assistant coaches. A washer and dryer arrived for their laundry, and a television and a video game system for their long nights stuck in the building. Living essentials: underwear, toothbrushes, and a change of clothes, which many of them did not have, trickled in. At times, quality was an issue, like when the boxers pulled on their boxing shoes and they ripped right through. Their headgear and gloves weren't even made for boxing, being clearly marked Taekwondo on all the pieces. For a while, he seemed like a swimming coach without a pool, but with each arrival of equipment, the Iraqi Olympic boxing center took shape.

The absence of equipment did not impede training, just altered it. The first week, in the absence of even a punching bag or gloves, he concentrated on the development of two things: their mindset and their condition. Prior to their morning roadwork in the basketball gym, he gathered the group on the

83

bleachers each day for team meetings. Termite fed their minds a steady, powerful stream of positive thoughts. He spoke slowly to allow the interpreter adequate time, "You deserve this opportunity. Opportunity has knocked on your door, and you need to seize this moment. You are the new role models for your country." Looking into their eyes, he emphasized, "You can do this. You are the best fighters your country has, and you have the opportunity to travel the world representing your country, to see your flag raised in Athens." Always mindful of the torture many athletes endured under Uday Hussein, he added, "It's not about winning or losing, it's about doing your best, having fun and enjoying boxing. Do you know *why* we're going make this happen?" He repeated the question loudly, "Do you know *why* we're going to make this happen? A huge grin covered the coach's face. "Because," he clapped his hands rhythmically, "Iraq…is back. Iraq is back. Iraq…is back…."

The smaller weight classes always jumped up first, due to better knees or better rhythm, and danced with their coach. The heavyweights shuffled with less enthusiasm, but everyone got up. Circling the gym, the chant grew louder, echoing in the metal building. In a small basketball gym far from Athens, an Olympic team began the bonding process. Termite hugged them, he praised them, he kissed them, he motivated them, and he pushed them.

Termite and the three Iraqi coaches who joined the team worked the boys hard, gut-wrenchingly hard. They knew how dangerous it was for out-of-shape boxers in the ring and their boxers had not worked out for months, some hadn't even fought in two years. The Iraqi team would soon face highly conditioned boxers at the Olympic qualifiers, strong athletes with fast feet and hands – athletes capable of hurting his boys. Their coach laid out the painful commitment required now in training that could protect them later. He explained to them, "I'm going to hurt you today and every day in this gym – I'm going to hurt you because I love you and I want you to be your very best. Outside this gym, I'm your best friend; inside this gym, I'm your worst enemy." They understood. Twenty-four boxers, each with a dream, pressed their physical limits every day.

Anything he asked, they did. Termite wanted so much to rouse something in them, to stir them, to inspire them to reach higher. But *his* were the eyes welled with tears, *his* was the heart inspired to do anything for his boxers, these big-hearted men who had traveled from all over the country to train with a stranger, an uninhibited American who danced around the gym.

With forty-three days left before the first qualifier in the Philippines, the Fatima Al-Zahra catering company arrived early to set up for the event. More than one hundred guests were expected at the official kick-off of the Iraqi Olympic boxing team. Local dignitaries, Iraqi newspapers and television stations, community leaders, and CPA members streamed through the double doors of the training center. It was an evening filled with pride. All eyes were immediately drawn to the new, just delivered boxing ring, with a real canvas floor and ropes. Heavy bags, speed bags, and jump rope platforms constructed by a KBR carpenter outlined the circuit training system the boxers already knew as a routine. Just two weeks from the day Termite had slammed his hand down in Baghdad demanding to know the whereabouts of his boxers, they were here, putting on a boxing exhibition for the community of Hilla.

The crowd pressed around the ring as Mr. Gfoeller's large frame ambled between the ropes of the ring. Mr.Gfoeller, dressed in his trademark safari vest, khaki pants, and fedora, welcomed the predominately male crowd in Arabic, acknowledging dignitaries and members of the Iraqi Boxing Federation, who had driven down for the event. Congested behind him were twenty-four boxers, three Iraqi assistant coaches, and Termite. Mr. Gfoeller turned the program over to Termite, whose remarks were translated by Mahawi Shibley, a highly regarded Iraqi assisting coalition leaders in southern Iraq.

Termite looked out on the crowd, and realized that this was a most unusual situation for an American to be in. The fact that the armed U.S. military was posted at every corner of the building inside and out underscored the unique nature of the evening. His country occupied their country; he would coach their men.

The coach relied on a theme that every Iraqi understood – obstacles. "We have a long way to go before Athens." Termite started, spreading his arms out expressively. Mahawi repeated the phrase with the exact gesticulation, facial expression, and tone. "There will be so many obstacles along our way, but we will always find a way around those obstacles." Mahawi communicated the message in Arabic, and Termite noticed heads nodding in agreement. "You will see in a moment that the Iraqi boxers have tremendous hearts, the biggest hearts in the world." Muhawi placed his hands over his heart, just as Termite had done. "These men have tremendous ability and will continue to work very hard on their conditioning in the gym. Now…" he paused for Mahawi to catch up. "…we are going to show you that…" As Termite's smile broadened, so did Mahawi's, "Iraq…is back. Iraq is back. Iraq…is back…" The men clapped their hands, and the boxers joined in. The coaches, Mahawi, and twenty-four Olympic athletes danced around the perimeter of the ring. The shout of "Iraq is back!" shot out to the caterers, the old boxing federation, local politicians, and coalition and KBR employees.

The crowd, mostly in traditional robes but some in business suits, was unaware of the meaning of the chant, but they smiled – somewhat confusedly- but they all smiled. The boxers, in their brightly colored mix and match tank tops and shorts celebrated their arrival to the world of international sports. They could travel outside of Iraq, something few Iraqi athletes were ever permitted to do; they could lose a match and not fear physical retribution against themselves or their families. They could just be athletes, sportsmen, and boxers.

The sparring began with the lightweights and proceeded through the weight classes to the super heavyweights. Their skills were rusty, but their passion for the sport was apparent. Energetic applause erupted after each bout. Termite positioned himself at the corner of the ring, part referee and part coach. Mahawi leaned over the ring with him. "Stick with your jab!"

the coach shouted. As the last syllable sounded, Mahawi instructed the boxers in Arabic, with the same intensity and clenched fist as the coach. "Keep your chin down!" Termite instructed. The command came quickly in Arabic. "Cut off the ring!" Termite exclaimed, slicing his hand through the air. The same authoritative tone and hand gesture echoed from Mahawi. Mahawi, a dignified Middle Eastern version of Sean Connery, had a commanding presence, and the boxers immediately responded to his voice. At the conclusion of the exhibition, the Iraqi team mixed with the crowd, answering questions and posing for the cameras.

Mr. Gfoeller, flanked by his ever-present security detail, approached Termite. Abundantly enthusiastic about the turnout and community support for the team and the coach, he spoke softly, "Termite, you know that Mahawi is a top aide." He paused in the same manner as the day he informed him of his new coaching title. "Termite, I'm going to give you Mahawi to assist you with the team. There's one condition - just take good care of him for me." Termite's reluctance showed. Mahawi was a well-educated engineer and former executive of an Iraqi oil company who was immensely valuable to the coalition in navigating political and cultural issues. His stately demeanor, probably due to the fact that he was a leader of a tribe of over one million Iraqis near Basra, his British accent, his affinity for business – none of these attributes added up to being aligned with a boxing team. Plus, a couple of months ago, Termite was killing the bugs in Mahawi's office – he was uncomfortable delegating tasks to a man of such importance. "Termite," Mr. Gfoeller said, "Mahawi is the right man for this job."

A man of vision, Mr. Gfoeller understood that hope for a nation could come in an unusual package. For Iraq, it just might be a boxing team. He also sensed that there would be times when Termite might need Mahawi to help negotiate some tight spots in the coming months. Termite needed more than an interpreter, he needed a partner.

Since good news was so scarce in Iraq, the television stations ran the story about the boxing team seven or eight times

87

a day, making Termite's face recognizable to many in Iraq. The team got back to training the next morning; back to overcoming hurdles in conditioning and technique.

One political hurdle loomed large. Amid all of the hoopla over the Olympic team, one glaring fact remained: Iraq was currently under a suspension from the International Olympic Committee due to Uday Hussein's treatment of the country's athletes. As it stood now, Iraqi athletes could not even compete in the games, regardless of their skill level. Termite wrote e-mails to the International Olympic Committee, pleading the case for the Iraqi athletes. Others did the same, most notably Mark Clark, the UK's senior sports advisor in Iraq. The team was heading into November of 2003; the first qualifier was in January 2004. Time was against them.

Politics of a much nastier nature came in the package of the former Iraqi Boxing Federation president, Saeed Abdelalhusin. The man who attempted to stonewall him in Baghdad about the whereabouts of the team, the man who refused to let Najah get on the bus to Hilla, was instigating trouble again. Slightly taller and twenty years older than Termite, Saeed wore western style clothes and dark sunglasses, even indoors. Shifty-eyed, he was reminiscent of a 1930's gangster guarding a gambling operation. He was being squeezed out of Iraq's amateur boxing program, a separate entity from the Iraqi Olympic Committee, but his demeanor revealed not a hint of acceptance of that fact. Saeed tested Termite's resolve and patience, making unrealistic demands to establish his fading authority.

An early conflict emerged when Saeed sent his own son as the sole representative in the 60K weight class, avoiding a box-off for the first team spot. Saeed's son Emad was a personable, handsome, kid with a great disposition, but Termite wanted to send the best boxers in Iraq, not the sons of those with clout. When questioning Saeed about where the other boxer was in his weight class, he would only reply, "My son will be going." Termite tried to appeal to a sense of fair play, "We need to give other fighters an opportunity, and if he's the best, he can go." Termite lost that battle, simply because he did not have the resources to find another fighter. Emad paid at practice. Even though the 132-pound boxer frequently apologized for his father's behavior, the Iraqi coaches and boxers gave him less respect than others whom they knew deserved the spot. Termite implored, "Work with Emad, he shouldn't pay for his father." Saeed didn't make his son's life any easier when, on visits to the gym, told the boxers, "Don't listen to the American, I am president of the boxing federation."

The days of treating Saeed like an out-of-control little league dad were quickly ending. Apparently frustrated over his loss of control, he informed Termite that one of the boxing federation members staying in the gym would be removed, and that he would now be taking their subsidy. The federation itself in Baghdad had selected those resident members, and Termite had a good rapport with these men. They handled some of the behind the scenes work: passport issues, equipment, phone calls, and they were highly supportive of the team.

"Saeed," Termite demanded, "Are you going to live here in the gym and take care of the team like these men have been doing?" He knew the response. Saeed felt the money was owed to him as president; he had no intention of working for it. When Termite refused to replace a federation member with Saeed, he made another demand – that he would instead replace one of the Iraqi coaches. Termite asked him, "Are you going to get up at night when one of the boys is sick? Are you going to be with us in the gym at 5:30 in the morning?" Termite would not budge; the team, including coaches and federation members, was in place and he would not be bullied.

Saeed's demands only relented briefly. Termite received a phone call from Saeed requesting a meeting. Mark Clark was down from Baghdad on business for the Ministry of Youth and Sports; Termite asked Mark to sit in on the meeting that was destined to be contentious. Mark, Termite, Mahawi, and Saeed gathered around the old wooden desk in the office adjacent to the gym.

Termite set the opening tone with remarks about "Doing the right thing for the boys," and then asked Saeed his purpose for the meeting. Saeed announced that he was going to now replace both of the federation members and Najah Ali, the boxer who shared his Olympic plans with Termite on the soccer field in Baghdad. As Muhawi translated Saeed's declaration into English, Termite's pulse raced. "If you have a better fighter than Najah, bring him here and we'll see if he can beat him – can he beat him?" Termite asked. Saeed talked around the subject, refusing to answer. "Can he beat Najah?" Termite demanded to know. "No," Saeed replied. Incredulous about what Saeed had just said, the tone in Termite's voice went from "Let's all get along" to total frustration. "Then why in the world would you replace Najah if he's the best fighter?" Mahawi's translation to Arabic showed the same tense nature. "That's just how we do business," Saeed responded smugly.

Termite felt the heat in his face, "Well, that's not how *I* do business. We're going to have the best team available to represent Iraq in the qualifiers. Najah is the Arab Champion in his weight class, so if you don't have a better boxer, he's going!" As the translation processed in his mind, Saeed's face became increasingly bellicose. His next set of demands streamed out, "I'm going to remove both of the federation members and Najah." Termite's temper was on the brink of being unleashed. He demanded, "Why do you want to remove these men who have worked so faithfully for the team and for me?" Saeed watched Mahawi as he interpreted. "Because I am going to go in their place to the Philippines and I am bringing a photographer with me." On his best diplomatic day, Mawahi could not have prevented Termite's next response. "Get out of my gym, Saeed, you are no longer welcomed here! I will put you out of any capacity in boxing in Iraq. Stay away from my boxers, and stay away from this gym!" Termite rose from behind the desk to conclude the meeting.

Saeed got up slowly and deliberately from the old vinyl chair and walked quietly from the gym. Termite, Mark, and

Mahawi watched him exit, but all three knew that the bubble of deep resentment Saeed had just buried would rise again.

It was easy to understand the animosity Saeed had against the American coach, but it was much later that Termite pieced together the bitterness Saeed had against Najah. Najah was as gregarious as he was hard working, held a bachelors degree in computer science, and was one of Termite's top three fighters. The animosity stemmed from the fact that Najah had fought in competing boxing clubs from the ones Saeed managed, and the young fighter had beaten some of Saeed's best boxers. The twenty-three year old boxer's father was a former champion in Iraq, and had also chosen to fight in another club. If anyone was going to represent Iraq in the Olympics, it would be one of Saeed's boxers – he wanted Najah out.

What Termite could not do to Saeed, democracy did. Across the country, the first democratic elections in thirty-five years of Hussein rule were taking place, but not in political precincts. Members of sports federations and clubs cast ballots for new leaders in over five hundred elections. The first seeds of democracy sprouted at athletic clubs from Basra to Mosul. Saeed was cast out by his own members, and a new president was elected. His son Emad remained in Hilla and trained for the Philippines.

The team's rough edges became a little smoother each day in training. The coaches focused on improving boxing techniques that would score points in the ring. Judging would be done by five ringside men with a computerized system in which three out of five had to signal a punch at the very same time for it to register. Therefore, Termite emphasized straight punches that visibly made the head pop back so the judges would readily see and 'click' a hit. Similarly, they worked on bending their knees and punching upward to force the backward head movement. The men learned proper positioning of their bodies to better evade punches. The Iraqi boxers generally squared up to their opponents, opening up their entire body to hits. Termite's men had to alter their stance by leading with their shoulders or they would learn first hand the old boxing adage, "Kill the body and the head will follow."

Muhawi so frequently translated Termite's instructions to "Point with your shoulder, keep your chin down, and keep your hands up," that the Texan learned them in Arabic, albeit with a drawl. The fact that Iraqi athletes had not been competing internationally weakened them. The experience level of western fighters heading to Athens was high partly due to fighting experience; some boxers had fought more than two hundred bouts as opposed to an average of thirty fights for an Iraqi boxer. An exhibition against boxers in Karbala, a city northwest of Hilla on the Euphrates River, provided some experience, but Termite needed to get them out of Iraq so they could spar against higher caliber boxers. Trapped in Hilla, they could only spar against each other – they needed to box against a wider variety of styles before Athens.

Concrete concepts of boxing were mixed every day with messages of hope and freedom for their country. Mahawi's status and influence with the boxers enhanced the significance of the message. He viewed the coalition presence as liberation and a rare opportunity for Iraqis to govern themselves after so many years of persecution under a dictator.

The streets of Iraq; however, were anything but free. Even daily roadwork times were staggered for security reasons. Their head coach's high media visibility magnified the target on his back for the bad guys. Any walks down the streets for Termite included a bulletproof vest and shooters at each elbow. After the first month, he allowed his boys to run short errands for items needed at the gym. He could not accompany his boxers because he had to arrange security every time he left the compound or gym. He proclaimed over and over to his team, "One day, we'll be able to walk down the streets of Hilla, hand in hand, and not worry about getting shot." Mahawi would add, "Some day, *Insha'Allah.*" Termite agreed, "Some day, God willing."

Baghdad streets were far more dangerous than those around Hilla, and frequent trips for team related business underscored that fact. Departure times were never set for fear of word getting out via interpreters. At the last minute, those in the compound who needed to travel into Baghdad were simply told to "Load up!" Traveling over the Hilla River near the compound, the convoys traveled bumper to bumper to avoid infiltration. Passing a nearby village, old rusty Iraqi tanks from the first Gulf War were strewn alongside the roads. In the next village, children played on the defunct tanks like children in the states would pretend to drive a broken-down tractor. Closing in on the highway to Baghdad, they passed an intersection with a huge defaced picture of Saddam Hussein, and then accelerated northward towards Baghdad.

Flying through the open desert, the only green was the bright grass around the date trees. Moving past small villages, the poverty of the region around Hilla was rampant. Covered women in black worked in the ruthless heat in front of one-room huts just yards from the highway as perpetually barefooted children played nearby. Some of the poorest families had homes constructed of fabric sewn together and supported by poles. Their only valuable assets were the cows restrained near the homes. Small woven canopies of date palm leaves shielded the men from the sun as they visited, sitting cross-legged or in chairs. In some cases, Iraqis along the route opened war-related businesses. Bayonets from Russian-made AK-47's were the most popular items for sale. Regardless of the nature of the accumulation of men along the highway, the flow of adrenalin in the vehicle increased when numbers of Iraqi men were gathered.

A sharp contrast existed between the barren, poor desert communities south of Baghdad to the city itself. Homes became larger and more comfortable the closer the proximity to Baghdad. Rural areas of Iraq still identified with their villages and tribal leaders; city dwellers were more reliant on the Iraqi government. The bleak colors of horrific poverty were replaced by expansive modest neighborhoods intermingled with spectacular mosques and impressive academic institutes. Men mingling on the streets dressed predominately in slacks and shirts; the heads of the women remained covered, but often times with a simple scarf.

The proximity to the city limits of Baghdad sharply increased the danger to the occupants of every convoy. Traffic and innovative explosive devices (IED's) were the two primary causes for the stiff tension. At speeds of over 100 MPH, the lead car in the convoy, at the first sight of a traffic jam entering Baghdad, turned the convoy around and returned to Hilla. Halted traffic gave insurgents an opportunity to surround the car and open fire on everyone in it. In one case, Termite's convoy was ordered to stop by the U.S .military. They had discovered an IED lodged between the concrete joints of a Baghdad overpass just in front of their vehicles. Another trip was less fortunate. Inventive insurgents had placed a decoy IED in the roadway and an active explosive nearby. A vehicle in front of them swerved to miss what they thought was an IED and triggered the actual IED. Termite's convoy sped around the explosion and continued on toward the Green Zone. Some IED's were encased in soft drink cans, so every item in the roadway was suspect, and every cluster of Iraqi men staring down from overpasses or out from yards was suspect as well.

The transition from the Red Zone to the Green Zone required visitors to undergo an incredibly rigorous security gauntlet that began with eye-to-eye contact with U.S. tank and Humvees loaded with .50 caliber machine guns. Iraqi workers went through a different entrance and more stringent processes; however, even American workers were searched upon entry. Protected by razor wire, concrete walls, helicopters, and tanks, once inside the secure region, coalition workers could breathe easier after the stressful trip into Baghdad.

Like a separate town, it was sometimes called "The Bubble" because the thousands of coalition employees living there drove freely in the cordoned off area, swam in Hussein's pool, and ate at restaurants in the zone while right outside the walls chaos often erupted. The Green Zone consisted in part of Saddam Hussein's main palaces, presidential complexes, the convention center, and the al-Rashid Hotel, which now served as housing for coalition military and employees. The opulence of the main palace never dulled for Termite. The marble, looping stairways and magnificent gold chandeliers were stunning examples of the bilking of national resources while the bulk of the nation lived in dire poverty. The gold toilet handles and faucets evoked memories of the thirsty children he encountered throughout southern Iraq, children he and the team passed bottles of water to every day to at the gym.

Paul Bremer, the head of the coalition, enthusiastically supported the team. Termite and the team traveled to meet Mr. Bremer in one of the luxurious conferences rooms of the palace. The coach and the team presented him with an "Iraq is back!" T-shirt and cap in a conference room of the main palace. Mr. Bremer beamed when the team broke out in their now trademark "Iraq is back!" chant. It was just as important for the boxers, who were primarily from Baghdad, to see the lifestyle of the former dictator while the people, particularly the Shi'a population in the South, suffered.

Work in Hilla progressed. The coalition continued improving the lives of the area citizenry blacktopping roads and training Iraqi workers. The coaching staff began the process of selecting their first team for the Philippines. After roadwork and breakfast one morning, Mr. Gfoeller approached Termite with a simple, "Come, go with me." Getting into the Suburban, Termite could view Mr. Gfoeller's ever-present pistol in its holster. Traveling into the countryside of Hilla, the blacktopped roads turned into dirt. The short, solemn drive opened into the village of Al-Mahawil.

Traveling down a somewhat desolate road, small children ran alongside the Chevy. The road opened into a desert field with rows and rows of sand mounds. Termite and Mr. Gfoeller exited the Suburban. As far as his eyes could see, burial mounds rose a few feet from the desert plain. Termite walked alone through the mass graveyard where thousands had been murdered by Saddam Hussein's henchmen. One mound had the sandals of an entire family on the heap: two tiny sandals and two parents' sandals. The horrible reality hit him, "Who died first? Which ones in the family had to watch the others die?" The terror in the children's eyes had to be overwhelming. Some mounds only had weather-beaten shreds of clothing held down by rocks. A forensic expert staying at the compound told him that most had been shot, but many were decapitated. Such a lack of dignity in their last moments for a people he had grown to love. He was so profoundly disturbed and so deeply hurt that he just knelt and cried in the desert sand. The fact that this was just one of many sites around Hilla alone, and that mass graves like this were scattered throughout the country magnified his grief.

It was a tormented moment of recognition. He had spoken for weeks about rights and freedom to his team. He had always been confident in his country's mission in Iraq and was proud of the military. But, it was only at that moment that Termite really understood freedom. These thousands of Shi'as in Hilla were murdered wholesale for an attempted uprising against Saddam in 1991 after the first Gulf War. They were murdered because they dared to speak out against the government. They were dragged out of their homes and shot and beheaded in front of family members. As the hot breeze wafted across this site of a horrific mass murder, he connected with the history of his country and the thousands of deaths in so many wars to protect that speech. Freedom had been such an easy motivational tool for his boxers, but their teacher had just learned its real meaning.

He had come to Iraq to support the military in protecting American's rights and way of life. Termite hadn't counted on falling in love with these most gracious people, people who thanked soldiers and workers on the streets. People who welcomed him into their homes and shared any food they had. Resolution crept into his mind. Freedom was worth dying for. He was willing to die for the Iraqi people. Back in the states there was a swelling frustration over the location of Iraq's weapons of mass destruction. As he stood near the bodies of so many innocent Iraqis, he was proud of his country for freeing other Iraqis from the fate these poor victims had endured. All that was left behind of their destruction was fabric and sandals and bones, but hope for real freedom was here now for the relatives of these victims.

Shortly after the visit to the mass grave, Mahawi readied himself to discuss with the community doctor the possibility of ongoing medical exams for the boxers, who were pushing their bodies so hard. Termite offered, "I'll go with you." Mahawi heavily cautioned against that idea since Termite had not ordered any security detail. "Mahawi, we're always telling the boys that some day we will be able to walk down the street hand in hand. Let's you and I make that day today." Mahawi only responded, *"Insha'Allah."* Termite agreed, *"Insha'Allah."* Together they strode, hand in hand, to the doctor's office in downtown Hilla, past hundreds of Iraqis. Termite, since his first time becoming Iraq's unlikely Olympic coach, walked without machine-gunned bookends or a bulletproof vest. He felt uniquely safe in the midst of Iraqi citizens. Mahawi, in his address only reserved for those he cared about, softly emphasized, "My dear, we need to get back now." Termite agreed. Freedom moved at a slow pace in Iraq.

8

A Crazy American Goes to the Philippines

The Olympic boxing team of Iraq had trained as hard as their big hearts and worn bodies could handle. The soles of their new shoes had clocked hundreds of miles in the small circle of the basketball gym in Hilla. They'd sparred each other so many times in their new ring that the outcomes were predictable. All of the excruciating work was based on the hope, a miracle really, that the International Olympic Committee would allow Iraq to rejoin the world's athletes in Athens. This incredibly optimistic Texan had sold them on the idea that it would happen – that they would make it happen. With only two weeks left before the first Olympic qualifier, doubts crept into every boxer's mind. If their "Iraq is back!" chorus ended now, they would return to jobs in furniture factories and ice cream trucks. Termite and others had pled their case to the IOC; time was running out for the team. He was powerless to close the deal; days flew by as he awaited word.

Termite closed the e-mail from Mark Clark and cried. He cried for his team, for himself, and simply because his nine-month stay in Iraq had molded him into a more emotional man. He called his boys and Mahawi into the cramped office in the Hilla gym. Looking solemnly at his shoes, Termite detailed their journey from the soccer field in Baghdad to the team they were today and expressed his love and gratitude for the team and coaches. He recalled the "One chance in a million" shot their own coach had once calculated. Termite's feigned sadness gave into a huge grin as the coach looked up and exclaimed, "We're in!" The office erupted into sheer exuberance as a group dance circled around the desk, "Iraq is back...Iraq is back!" The once barefooted team with the makeshift ring now had the opportunity to get a boxer qualified for Athens. The boxer turned exterminator turned car salesman was right – they *had* found a way.

Termite impulsively said, "Guys, this is how we do it in America." The coach extended his hands out and his team fell in line. The office fell silent. Termite thanked God for allowing this opportunity to happen and asked God's blessing on their upcoming travel to the Philippines. Mahawi translated the prayer. It was a unique moment. Iraqi men were accustomed to unrolling their mats and falling into almost a trance-like state, this was a new experience for them. It seemed surprisingly natural; for above all, they were a team. From that point on, they prayed individually, but they prayed together at team meetings. Termite had such a great respect for their religion, but he wanted to share short spiritual moments with them as well, just as most athletes did around the world with their coaches.

As that huge obstacle of the sanction crashed down, another wall quickly appeared – how would he get his boxers out of Iraq to compete against the world? No commercial jets flew into or out of Iraq, only military jets. Travel options were sparse: a sixteen-hour bus ride to Jordan in a war zone or an eight-hour drive to Kuwait in similar conditions. Termite and Mahawi headed to Kuwait to lay the groundwork for getting the team out of Iraq. Driving across the desert, both men pondered the slim chances of receiving even a tepid welcome in a country that Iraq had brutally invaded in recent history. Kuwait did not allow Iraqis to travel in their country – could they persuade them to make an exception for the boxers?

Sheik Fahed, president of the Kuwait Olympic Committee, received them with such sincerity that immediate hope rose in Termite's veins. Dignified in his white headdress fastened with a brown wool cord, the sheik's fluent English and warm personality put the American stranger quickly at ease. The opening minutes of the welcome gave the coach a new perspective of the importance Mahawi held in the region. The entire Olympic delegation knew of Mahawi's reputation as a respected tribal leader and oil executive from Basra and listened intently to his opinions.

The rapport between Mahawi and the Kuwaitis deepened faster than the sheik's black Mercedes sped through the streets of Kuwait City. The discussion in the car, generally in English but at times reverting to Arabic, was on life before Saddam Hussein when the two peoples were not divided. Common blood lines throughout Kuwait and Iraq were established and all nodded at the tragedy of families in the two countries being split by the long-standing political situation. By the time the group arrived at the restaurant, phrases such as "Our brothers in Iraq" and "Rejoining our nations" were being used.

Termite reflected throughout the evening at the wisdom of Mr. Gfoeller's decision to assign Mahawi Shipley to a struggling boxing team rather than a high-level business negotiation. Mahawi's presence gave the team an Arabic gravitas required for the occasion. Without the Kuwaitis' blessings, travel to the Olympics was impossible and their dreams would literally not get off the ground. But these were Mahawi's boys now, too, and Termite knew that they were all in good hands.

The restaurant was like nothing the American had ever experienced. A waiter was assigned to each of the six men in the group. After feasting on goat, veal, and beef tips, the sheik motioned to the waiter for the nargile or hookah to be placed on the ornately designed table. Four elaborately designed water pipes with attached hoses arrived. The sheik first inhaled through the hose of his individual three-foot tall pipe; Mawahi followed suit and commented on the fine quality of the tobacco and mint mixture. Termite hadn't smoked anything since the Marlboro's he'd sneaked puffs on in the woods of North Shore, but he certainly did not want to offend the sheik at this delicate point in the discussion of his team. The American inhaled vigorously three or four times to get the smoke up the hose and then passed the hose back to Mahawi. Every time the hose returned to him, he inhaled deeply. Termite fielded occasional questions about his team, but found it increasingly difficult to concentrate. Lighter and lighter headed, he felt his weight press against the high backed chairs as the pipe gurgled relentlessly. His head swung like a slow pendulum from the Sheik to Mahawi as he tried to focus on the proceedings. In the dark, smoky restaurant, the sheik extended his hand to the coach, "Termite, we'll do whatever is needed to get your team into Kuwait. They are welcomed here." His woozy brain cleared fairly quickly at those words, and he thanked the delegation. Mahawi turned to Termite and said simply, "My dear, it is time for us to go."

The sheik assigned two men to make it happen, the one with the earliest significance was Ali Belushi, a beloved former heavyweight king of Kuwait. Now middle-aged, he was still recognized everywhere he and Termite went on the streets. Physically imposing but with a teddy bear's heart, the two former boxers bonded immediately. Generally meeting in Belushi's apartment, they primarily discussed travel and hotel arrangements; however, Ali and Termite also deliberated on shirts and pins for the team. One shirt designed by Belushi and produced in Kuwait said "I Love Iraq." A simple message for most countries, few in the world shared in that sentiment at that moment. Termite had no reservations about the statement – he wanted his men to rejoice in their patriotism; after all, he shared those passionate feelings for his own country. Belushi loved helping Termite and the team. These were just fellow boxers who needed support and he was just the man to provide it. Transportation issues, food, training facilities – anything Termite needed, Ali supplied.

Termite and Mahawi returned to Iraq with much more than they ever thought possible. The Iraqi boxers could not only travel through Kuwait to the Philippines, they had an invitation to train there during the week leading up to the qualifier. Termite returned home to Hilla to inform his team and coaches, and then headed to Baghdad with a mission. The growing insurgency, marked by car bombs and mortar attacks, made a long bus ride to Kuwait increasingly perilous for a high profile team traveling with an American. Having his boys blasted off the road to Kuwait was no longer an option. Termite now wanted the U.S. military to transport the team into Kuwait.

The initial broaching of the request via e-mail went poorly. Mark Clark, the trusted Brit who worked with the Ministry of Youth and Sports, was brutally honest. It was "highly unlikely" that the U.S. would transport a group of Iraqi citizens into Kuwait. Sixty days would be required to even attempt such a mission - Termite had two weeks. In addition, his boxers lacked valid visas.

In the Green Zone in Baghdad, Termite stood at Mark's desk and reiterated the danger, saying, "Man, we've got to have that plane; I don't want the team to get shot at." The two men generated excitement about the project to the layers of the military. It was a surprisingly easy sell, because everyone in the military saw it as an opportunity to do an incredibly positive and historic thing for the nation of Iraq. Paul Bremer, always a supporter of the team, sanctioned the flight, although the decision was solely the military's.

Visas were rushed through as the Kuwaiti officials issued a letter providing permission to enter and train in the country. The military saw the noble purpose of treating the team "with due ceremony befitting an Olympic team representing their country." At every military level the boxers were viewed as "Ambassadors for the new Iraq." They had their plane. They had Kuwait on board as a base for commercial travel throughout the world. Loaded down with T-Shirts, Olympic pins, and an American "can-do" attitude, the world's most unusual Olympic team was ready to compete.

In early January 2004, the Iraqi entourage boarded the American military cargo plane. The magnitude of the moment was measured in the countless flashes from cameras held by military men and women. The team situated themselves in the mesh seating on the sides of the C-130 and flew the hour and a half to Kuwait. In Kuwait, they landed on the U.S. military base, were welcomed by the Kuwait delegation, and bussed to the Kuwait Residence Hotel. The newspapers in Kuwait heralded the historical significance of the team's presence and underscored the role the boxing team played in reuniting two nations separated by political strife.

Training in Kuwait, the team did their roadwork along the sea wall of the bay. It was the first time the team had run outside the confines of the close, sweaty gym. Just being able to stretch their legs on a path rather than turning in a tight circle was liberating to the athletes. The coach and team ate together at malls and shopped with virtually no security concerns. The nervous tension from the war receded momentarily and they focused on just being athletes preparing for the Olympics.

At the end of the tremendous week of Kuwaiti hospitality and training, an invigorated team arrived at the Kuwait airport three hours early for their commercial flight to Manila at 11:00 P.M. Upbeat and confident after being treated like world-class athletes for the week, the men proudly sauntered through the Kuwaiti airport and flashed their newly attained visas for security. Disappointedly, the new Olympic spirit between the two countries had not reached the security gates of the airport.

An immediate barrage of arrogant anti-Iraqi sentiment flowed from the security personnel. "You can't get on this plane," security repeatedly warned. "Your visas don't even show that you've entered Kuwait legally." Termite and Mahawi repeatedly justified that the visas were not stamped because the Olympic Committee escorted them right off the plane on a U.S. base straight to their hotel and skipped routine procedures. The coach kept imploring them to contact the sheik, but that request just brought scorn and laughter from the security staff.

Hours rolled by and the team was continually refused admittance to the plane. Repeatedly, security demanded an answer to the same question, "How did you get into Kuwait?" Termite tried over and over again, "Look, Sheik Fayed," he began again, but each attempt brought rolled eyes and smirks by the security staff. "Yeah, right, you know the sheik, they laughed." The team finally stretched out on the floor and chairs of the airport and slept. Termite checked the wall clock every few minutes. Mahawi's keen and persistent negotiating skills failed to impress the security staff. The boarding announcements began for the flight to the Philippines and the team looked at their coach with panicked expressions. Termite's tone intensified as he pleaded, "I have to have these boxers on that plane."

Right at 11:00, Mahawi's cell phone rang. "Termite, you have a phone call," Mahawi said. "Termite, this is Sheik Fayed, I'm so sorry about this. We're going to take care of this. Don't worry about the plane, we'll hold it for you." Termite extended his hand out to the security staff that had harassed them for three hours, saying, "You've got a phone call." After six or seven humble, "Yes, sirs," security looked at Termite and said in disbelief, "That was Sheik Fayed. Get your luggage and run as fast as you can for the gate."

The daily roadwork came in handy, as the Iraqi entourage sprinted down the airport. Montesor, the second Olympic committee member assigned to help the team, arrived to personally stamp their visas as they boarded the plane. Termite waited until the last boxer boarded and then, as soon as he stepped into the plane, the door closed and the plane jolted from the gate.

From the team's inception, he'd told them they would find a way. In Kuwait, Sheik Fayed supplied that way, holding up a planeload of business executives for a ragtag team headed to their first Olympic qualifier. The team's hurt feelings mended slightly when, once airborne, fellow passengers approached them for autographs. Termite's focus shifted to the next big obstacle: getting a boxer qualified.

The final warm-up for the games in Manila brought an onslaught of media coverage that was overwhelming at times. In Iraq, Reuters, Fox, CNN, and others covered the team, but in a manageable way in which the coach could handle the athletes' distractibility. Friendly but persistent, these reporters arrived in hordes before breakfast and stayed all day, following them on runs and eating meals with them. Over and over the team was asked, "How is it working with the American coach?" Over and over, the coach was asked, "How is it working with the Iraqis?" Occasionally, they would field pointed political questions about the U.S. invasion. The boxers, in individual terms, told about their newfound freedom and their deep concerns that the U.S. would leave the country.

Their week in Manila complete, the team flew in Palawan, a tropical resort island in the Philippines for the tournament. Flying over the plethora of islands and teal waters, they spotted a tiny runway that seemed impossible to land a plane on, and all their faces filled with concern. A culture away from Iraq and the Middle East, they deplaned on the small runway and were quickly approached by beautiful women in grass skirts who gently wrapped their necks in leis. Live native music pulsating through the tiny airstrip, Termite reckoned silently, "My boxers are better equipped to handle incoming mortar attacks than women in grass skirts." He reckoned wrong. The Iraqi boxers laughed and joked as they swayed their butts to the live music. They had made it from a war-torn land to a plush island, and they welcomed the freedom to have some long-overdue fun.

From a war-ravaged country to a resort was a sizable cultural leap as well. In Iraq, men and women were accustomed to gender segregation. Schools were separated by girls and boys, and women's bodies remained significantly covered. Therefore, men in Iraq were used to recreational activities with just men and adjusted their behavior accordingly.

While checking in at the lobby desk, the boxers spied the indoor swimming pool and raced over, thrilled about the opportunity to swim. Termite glanced over from the registration counter and saw the entire team stripping down to their bikini underwear and diving into the pool. Termite darted over to the side of the pool, pushed aside mounds of clothing, and started to explain how things have to be different when women are around. He stopped. These guys had seen their cities bombed and cars burn. They deserved some fun and any minor embarrassment suffered by the staff was worth seeing them slash and dunk each other. Later in the week, Termite reserved massages for some of the boxers whose muscles were particularly sore. The single ones, having never been touched by a woman, requested that their coach remain with them. Termite positioned himself at the head of the two massage tables and "chaperoned" his boys. The next day, the two headed for another massage, but told the coach, "Thanks, but we don't need you this time."

They were the focus of a media extravaganza in Palawan. Their eyes blurred from camera flashes from the time they opened their doors in the morning to the last good nights. The competition team had eleven boxers – one for each division, but they were followed by twenty reporters on roadwork. Taking off down the village road in close proximity to designer laden China and Japan, the Iraq team wore whatever shorts they could scrape together – there were no sports logos on any of them. They returned to breakfast, lunch, and dinner with the media. Generally, reporters were genuinely interested in the obstacles the boxers and the coach had crossed to get to the qualifier; however, one Asian television reporter named Charmaine arrived with an axe to grind.

Walking up to the coach, she demanded, "Are you Mr. Watkins?" Termite nodded. "Well, I don't like you and I don't like Americans. America has no business being in Iraq and you have no business being Iraq's coach," she blasted. Termite gazed in stunned silence at the short young woman with the dark hair touching her shoulders. Her cameraman recorded the antagonism. "Unfortunately," she continued, "I have to interview one of your boxers for my station. Which one will you let me talk to?" Taken aback by her blatant hostility, Termite simply replied, "You can interview any of them – you decide." Obviously surprised, she confirmed, "You'll let me speak with any boxer?" Termite agreed. She pointed to Majeed – "I'll talk to *that* one."

Out of the entire team, Majeed was the last one Termite wanted the media to interview. "Why couldn't she pick Najah?" he thought, "His good-natured charm comes across immediately." It wasn't that Termite didn't like Majeed, it was that Majeed never smiled and rarely talked. The 113-pounder always looked like he was mad at the world, and he probably had good reason for the attitude, but the coach wanted the media coverage to be positive. At thirty-one years of age, Majeed knew this was his last opportunity and was struggling mightily to make weight for the tournament. His sour disposition was aggravated by hunger and nightly leg cramps.

Charmaine took Majeed aside for the interview, asking pointed questions about "that American" and the war. She returned the boxer to Termite and, showing open surprise, reported, "He loves you. He thinks of you as family." Charmaine systematically interviewed every single boxer on the team, every Iraqi coach, and Mahawi.

With each interview, her demeanor softened. Independently, each boxer spoke about what it felt like to be free to fight, and they expressed in their own words how much this American had done for them – from the soccer field to the Philippines. They described him as their friend, as their surrogate father, and as their beloved coach who gave them the opportunity to box internationally for the love of the sport. Equally importantly, the boxers inspired the somewhat cynical reporter, and she became a true friend of the team.

At the end of the interview gauntlet, she finally asked Termite for an interview. Termite agreed, but on the condition that he say his peace. She agreed to his terms. "Charmaine," he began, "I've stood in a mass gravesite with thousands of innocent Iraqis. I've seen little girls' shoes on top of those sandy mounds. Someone had to come to their rescue, and I'm proud that my country was the one to stand up to that dictator who murdered families in the middle of the night. You speak of Americans as something so negative, but Americans have given those men their freedom. You wouldn't be here interviewing them without America." He waited for her response and received silence in its place. "Now, let's start the interview."

His team was as fit and ready as he could get them in fifty-seven days. Their skills had improved dramatically from the long days of preparation, and he could not have been prouder of them. Something besides training had weighed on Termite's mind for the past week, and just hours before the opening ceremony, Termite revealed his concern. "I've decided not to march into the arena with you. This is your day, and it needs to be about you." Termite understood that an American in their midst often diverted media attention from the deserving team to the unlikely and colorful coach. They adamantly refused to accept his decision. Termite was their coach, their friend, and their mentor. He had fed them, clothed them, trained them, and befriended them. The consensus was "If you don't go, we don't go."

Emotions were soaring as they lined up by weight class preparing their entry into the small coliseum. No one could recall the last time an Iraqi boxing team had fought outside of their Middle Eastern neighborhood. The announcer emphatically stated, "The country of Iraq" and the crowd rose in a burst of applause. Entering two by two in their green and black nylon sweats, the smallest boxers entered first. Standing in the entrance, the chant began, "Iraq…is back. Iraq is back! Iraq…is back. Iraq is back!

Najah, weighing only 48 kilos and just shy of five feet tall, entered confidently. The tremendous pride the littlest boxer had in himself, his team, and his country was hugely apparent. From the soccer field in Baghdad, he had been the athlete to stop Termite and tell him that he would go to Olympics. Arriving in Hilla late after being refused admittance on the bus from Baghdad, he'd paid his own way to train with the American. He was a mighty man with an optimistic spirit that rivaled that of his coach.

Majeed walked proudly next to Najah. At 52 kilos, he was the second smallest of the travel team selected from the box-off in Hilla. In contrast to Najah, he rarely smiled and could sit stone faced during a mortar attack. Reserved and quiet, he was also forthright. When he spoke, he told his feelings so honestly he had changed the heart of the hard-spoken reporter. In his early thirties, his work ethic inspired the boxers and

108

coaches. His trouble making weight caused him to have to work off pounds, so when the other boxers were relaxing, Majeed was often running laps in layers of sweats.

Saraka entered the arena with tears streaming. Saraka had grown up poorer than the other boxers and saw boxing as a way to better his life in Iraq. One of the best in the country, his classy style reminded Termite of Sugar Ray Robinson. He threw a lot of punches in the ring and was accustomed to dominating his opponents. The boxer needed to be told that he was good in the ring, and his coach supplied that frequent recognition. This competition meant the world to the boxer.

Walking next to Saraka was Jassim, a proud boxer in his thirties. A quiet man, he exuded pride and dignity. Winner of every Arab title, any boxing fan in the Middle East knew the athlete's reputation. His age made this competition critical; he hoped to break through onto a new level of his career.

Emad boxed at 60 kilos. As the son of the former president of Iraq's boxing federation, the pressure to succeed was evident. Often feeling a lack of acceptance from the team, he used his talent for comedy to break through the circle of distrust placed by his father.

Fallah entered the arena with the same sweet countenance he'd exhibited throughout their journey. In his late twenties, he was not a good boxer by sheer athletic ability, but rather by tremendous work and discipline. Extremely handsome, he just seemed happy naturally, with an ever-present serene smile.

Looking and fighting in a style resembling Sugar Ray Leonard, Zuhair strode into the arena flashing his brilliant white smile. A talented boxer, the 152 pounder was a master of the Ali shuffle and could make boxers miss then pay repeatedly. Concerned in early practices that the coach would frown on his 'hot-dogging' moves, Termite alleviated his fears when he told him to "just have fun." Great confidence combined with a great attitude and skills made Zuhair one of the best on the team.

Marching proudly into the arena next to Zuhair was Ahmed, one of the most fun-loving members of the team.

Termite liked to play pranks on the team; Ahmed turned it around on the coach, usually by sneaking up on Termite and scaring him. One of the oldest on the team, he was the unofficial cheerleader, praising the others with a "We can do it!" His deep-seated eyes were determined – no matter how hard Termite pushed him, the boxer responded with his great attitude.

Iraq's heavyweight walked in with the same quiet dignity he had exhibited since the first day in Hilla. His scarred back from past beatings was a reminder to the team of sports under the old regime. At thirty-four, the maximum age for an Olympic boxer, Mohammed was a respected veteran of the team. Winner of thirteen Iraq national titles, he had never been allowed to go the Olympics. Win or lose, he was now free to just box for the love of the game. Win or lose, he would return home to Iraq to the two things that truly brought him joy – his two daughters.

Accompanying Mohammed was Ali, Iraq's super heavyweight. A kind, dear man with a huge grin, he could not escape the long shadow cast by his famous brother. A long-time heavy weight king in Iraq, his brother's celebrity status was such that people would stop him on the street to kiss his hand. Ali looked like a boxer who had been in one too many fights. His large nose had been broken so many times that it was flat and crooked, and several teeth were missing. Suffering from a lifetime problem with high blood pressure, the doctor in Palawan tried to prevent Ali from participating in the tournament. Fortunately, Termite had proactively secured a letter from an Iraqi doctor providing medical clearance for Ali.

His boxers walking in front of him, Termite entered with Mahawi. From the first day in Hilla, the boys had talked openly about their dream of seeing their flag raised in Olympic competition. Termite had never known that he could be so moved by another country's flag. This was for them, yet he felt such a privilege in just being with them. The so close title fight, the bloody comeback – somehow his own missed dreams faded into irrelevance as he brought new dreams to these deserving

110

boxers. A fourth of the way around the arena, the chant heard 'round the world erupted, but no one knew the source of its inception. "Iraq...is back, Iraq is back!" The crowd rose to their feet in a standing ovation for his boys. Win or lose, the purity of sports was, for a moment, intact.

Winning was, however, much sweeter. The opening round gave the Iraqis a big boost. Najah Ali, their smallest, most confident boxer, manhandled his opponent. Najah dropped him in the first round, and then continued to dominate round after round. At the start of the last round, Termite told him, "You've out pointed him so badly, son, just go out there and have some fun." Najah, excited about his impending win, dropped his hands and taunted him, but the boxer still could not hit him. Termite kept a mental count of points, and knew that Najah had at least a twelve-point lead at the final bell. Najah excitedly bounced up and down waiting for the referee to lift his glove as the victor.

Pure agony washed his face as his opponent's glove was raised. He pleaded to the referee and to Termite, "Something is wrong; this can't be right." Termite had never seen anything quite like it in a lifetime of boxing. He told his boxer, "I want *you* to continue to be a good sport, but I don't have to." Termite headed to the judges' table, leaving behind a tear-stained, devastated boxer standing next to the ring.

His boxer had been robbed, and Termite's anger pooled with each step towards the table of eight judges. The coach leaned over the table and gazed into the eyes of a middle aged Pakistani official, the son-in-law of Anwar Chowdry, president of the Federation of Asian Amateur Boxing. "I need some answers on Najah's fight. I want to see the score card." The slender Pakistani stared right back at Termite and ordered emphatically, "Sit down and shut up." There was no chance in a million that the coach would accept that command. Termite slammed his hand sharply on the table, "I'm not leaving until I see the score card for the fight. I've got a right to be here and I've got a right to see the score card." The Pakistani official snidely conceded to the other judges, "Show him." Termite read it with disbelief; 21-8 against Najah was the final point tally. "This is not right, Termite said, "The score is backwards – Najah beat the guy easily – the other guy didn't have a prayer."

Prior to this moment, Termite had brushed away whispered conversations in the arena about corruption in the games. "I want to file a protest." The Pakistani replied, "You can file a protest, but it will cost you $100.00." Termite fought the messages arriving in his brain, all of which involved the judge's head hitting the table. "What do I get for my $100?" Termite demanded. The official answered, "The other officials and I will sit here and talk it over and come up with a decision." Termite stood in front of them in total disbelief of what had transpired. Not only had they stolen Najah's fight, they now wanted money to talk about their crime. "I'm not giving you thieves any of my money." Termite said in disgust, and he turned to head back to Najah. He had to explain to the hardest working boxer on the team that the first Olympic qualifier was taken from him probably because of rampant corruption.

Immediately after telling Najah, Termite arrived ringside at Majeed's fight just in time to witness a barrage of punches to his Kuwaiti opponent. With the Iraqi coaches cheering him on from the corner, Majeed continued his relentless attack. The fight was stopped early and Majeed's hand was raised in Iraq's first victory to a standing ovation from the crowd. Termite's huge smile masked his distaste over the disturbing scene at the officials' table. His instincts told him that the tournament was tainted, and his brain searched for options that could protect his team.

The next fight in the opening day of the tournament was Saraka, was one if Iraq's top boxers. He'd risen from the poorest streets of Basra to work his way to the top of that country's ranks. From the corner, Muhawi interpreted Termite's instructions to the boxer. Saraka fought a great fight, doing everything his coach asked. He applied pressure when he needed to, and he moved and boxed when he had to. Saraka clearly and decisively won the fight, and stood in the center of the ring awaiting the announcement. As the other boxer's hand went up, Saraka dropped immediately to his knees. Crying out in Arabic, Saraka pounded the canvas with his fists. His chance to rise from poverty was taken. He rose to his feet and began running around the ring, raising his hands to the crowd in disbelief and sorrow. Termite and Mahawi rushed to his side in a futile attempt to console the boxer. In just their third fight of the tournament, the American coach felt powerless to help his team. In all their days of preparation, he had not prepared them for this. He knew that without a knockout or a sheer beating that forced a stoppage, they would get no decisions in the Philippines.

Seated between the two rings of the arena was Anwar Chowdry, a man Termite heard referred to with two nicknames, "The Dictator" and "The Godfather." He displayed his power boldly by sitting conspicuously in a high back chair brought in just for him. To his side was a leather sofa placed for his visitors. In his eighties, he walked with a cane and often with assistance from others. His body weak, he was entirely lucid and had a firm grip on the proceedings in the Olympic trial.

Over the next few days, the pieces of the corruption puzzle began fitting into place. Walking between the two rings, an official approached Termite and in a matter-of-fact tone, explained the boxing business in that part of the world. Flatly, he laid out the quid pro quo. "Bring gifts and money to Chowdry, and you'll get some of these decisions." Termite's eyes were instinctively drawn upwards to Chowdry's chair. "The Dictator" acknowledged Termite with a nod, confirming the coach's suspicions that the official had been sent specifically to get him in line with the unofficial rules. Angry at his fighters having their dreams snatched away by greed, he did not return the nod. Instead, the American pointed his finger towards Chowdry, positioned roughly twenty yards away. "You tell Chowdry that I'm not going to pay him nothing. He needs to pay *me* to keep my mouth shut, but he doesn't have enough money to do that." Termite glared at Chowdry and walked away, his veins throbbing with revulsion at the proceedings in the Philippines.

The reality of their boxing world provided Termite with an unfamiliar obstacle. Support came his way from many coaches and team leaders, weary of years of talent and skill losing out to bribery. As the seven-day tournament unfolded, more and more coaches came forward with the same story, generally approaching with a sincere, "Can we talk in private?" to Termite. They saw a man crazy enough to take a stand against a man everyone feared, and shared their stories about the corruption that had tainted a generation of boxers. Termite was not squeamish about taking that stand; he just needed a vehicle to mount the charge.

The vehicle for exposure was right in front of him at breakfast, lunch and dinner – Termite decided to use the powerful influence of the media to expose the underbelly of Asian amateur boxing. He turned the onslaught of reporters to his advantage and used the exposure of the corruption as protection for himself. Selecting his words carefully, he told reporters, "There are things going on here that shouldn't be going on here – they've got to stop." He repeated that message over and over to insure coverage and added. "I'm not going to play the games that go on here." Termite alluded to the lack of "integrity in the games."

That lack of integrity escalated as a top official confronted Termite at the hotel, telling him, "You're going against the grain. To get these decisions, you're going to have to take care of these referees and judges with money, gifts, or liquor." The vocal Texan was irate and retorted, "That will never happen with me. You're here to take care of these young men, not to benefit yourself." Mid-tournament, Termite tried to keep his emotions in check and to examine any possible way to win in a system loaded against an honest team.

Termite's increasing vocal opposition in the media combined with his firm stance against exchanging money for wins set up an inevitable clash with Chowdry. The system had been in place for years with few challenges. At the closing ceremonies, music, food, and dance filled the arena. Termite's team had little to celebrate in terms of wins, but a lot to celebrate in just being in international competition. As the night drew to a close, a board member approached Termite, "Termite, Professor Chowdry would like a word with you." The coach walked up to a table of about twenty individuals, all leaders in boxing from their prospective nations.

"Mr. Chowdry, you wanted to speak with me?" Termite asked in feigned respect. Chowdry coldly stared into Termite's eyes. "Don't you ever go to the media again." Before Chowdry could continue, the coach replied, "First of all, I don't have to go to the media, they come to me. Everywhere we go, they follow." Termite paused for a second. "Evidently," Termite continued, "You've got me wrong. You don't tell *me* what to do." Openly agitated, Chowdry fired, "Do you know who I am?" Termite nodded, "Yeah, you're a corrupt man." Chowdry reiterated, "Do you really realize who I am?" Shocked at the tone of the conversation, Termite turned the tables on the old man, "Do you realize who *I* am?" Termite demanded. Chowdry weighed his response and replied, "Yes, you're a crazy American who doesn't know what he's getting into. You're in way over your head, and you need to go home while you can." The intensity of their dialogue increased with every passing second. Termite demanded to know, "Is that a threat?" Chowdry admitted, "Yes, a personal one." Termite ended the discourse with a firm, "Your threats don't bother me, and I'm here to stay." The coach turned his back on Chowdry, returned to his team's celebration, and pretended not to notice the glares from "The Dictator's" delegation.

The nicknames rang true. Like a dictator he used threats and intimidation to control boxing matches. Free from the burden of Saddam, his team had been controlled by a dictator of another sort. Boxers from the Asian countries arrived with burning dreams, and left with hollow victories and disputed defeats. This crazy American with 128 amateur fights under his belt had taken a stand for every boxer who got into the ring and expected an honest bout.

Anxious to get home to Iraq to re-group and re-energize the team for the next qualifier in China, the boxers arrived for their Manila-Kuwait flight. Like a nightmare revisited, the team was refused boarding rights to the plane. Montesor, the Kuwaiti official who traveled into the Philippines with the team had left the day before with the Kuwait boxing team. Manila security informed them that, without a Kuwaiti official, they could not get on a plane and travel anywhere. An exhausted, frustrated team stretched across another cold airport floor, using their suitcases as pillows. Eight hours later, after forty or fifty calls, Sheik Fayed was located. A simple fax to the airport validating their entry into Kuwait provided the documentation.

Weary boxers filed into the plane and plopped into their seats desperate for rest. Dejected from the results in Palawan and tired from eight hours on an airport floor, they bore no resemblance to the boxers dancing at the airstrip with the grass-skirted girls. As soon as the plane took off, the television screens came on. With amazing timing, a documentary featuring the "Iraq is back" team detailed the obstacles the team had mounted to be in the qualifiers. Footage of the men dancing around their gym in Hilla to their famous chant lit up their faces. Even though they had no medals to take home, they were going home winners. These boxers had done what hadn't happened in Iraq in years – they had left Iraq and had fought in an international tournament. After signing autographs for passengers at the close of the documentary, they fell asleep.

They had been instrumental in mending fences with Kuwait, an old neighbor. They had marched into an arena with their flag held high. They had fought gallantly, regardless of the results. And they had battled airport security in two countries. It hadn't been easy, but Iraq was back.

116

9

A Light Goes Out in Iraq

The three soldiers, each laden with machine guns, formed a triangle around the coach as he walked into the Hilla gym. Inside he watched his boxers run the familiar circle around the floor; an additional armed soldier hovered over them as well. They had returned from the Philippines to a much tougher neighborhood. The population of Hilla, predominately Shiite, looked upon the Americans as liberators; unfortunately, the insurgency centered in Baghdad had spread into the Babylon region. The warm, trusting relationship between the coalition and their Iraqi neighbors had been carefully developed over the last nine months. The escalating insurrection strained those relationships.

Mortar and rapid-fire grenade attacks had become a near daily occurrence around the compound. Security was stretched increasingly thin to accommodate the hundreds of coalition and aid workers living in those gates. Travel was more treacherous than ever on the roads to Baghdad and Karbala. The already frayed nerves of the compound took a jolt on February 19, 2004. At 7:15 in the morning, a loud blast blew windows out of the building. As the workers scurried into the concrete bunkers behind the former hotel, smoke rose outside the camp, signaling the location of the blast. Military personnel took their positions around the perimeter and on the rooftops.

Only a quarter mile from the camp, two vehicles loaded with explosives had attacked the Polish camp, Camp Charlie. Alert Polish soldiers shot the driver of the first suicide vehicle; the second driver purposefully rammed into it, causing an explosion so immense that a crater sixty-feet wide and twenty-feet deep was carved into the desert road. Forty-four members of their coalition friends were wounded. Baghdad-style violence had arrived in relatively peaceful Hilla.

The escalating insurrection in Hilla troubled Termite more than his fighters, because their protection was his paramount responsibility. And, as Muslims, their philosophy of death was one of *Insha'Allah*; if God willed it, it was out of their hands anyway. The coach knew, based on many briefings, that his fighters were a target simply for being with him. Somewhat accustomed to gunfire and blasts from their years in Iraq, the boxers' nerves were practically unshakable. Termite's American nerves, however, still got rattled.

In the week following the car bombing, Termite and his team were standing just inside the gate of the gym area. Suddenly, a loud blast shook the complex. Termite instinctively and convincingly pushed the boxers into the gym, yelling "Get down!" The reluctant team balked, infuriating the coach, "Get under the bleachers! Get down!" Termite shoved members of his team under the bleachers; protecting them as best he could from the attack, continually yelling, "Take cover! Get down!" Termite made sure they were positioned safely, and then scrunched in next to them. Members of the team, perplexed at the coach's urgency, asked, "What is wrong with you, coach?" Termite repeated his warnings, "Stay down, get your heads down!" Huddled under the miserably hot bleachers together, one boxer finally got through to the coach. "Coach, that was just a transformer." It took several seconds for him to react, "Oh," he replied, a bit embarrassed, "Well, let's get back to practice, then."

The weight of keeping his team safe remained in Termite's thought processes every day, but another concern rose to the top of the mental pile. "What was going on with the Chinese?" he contemplated. In the final days of the Philippine qualifier, two Chinese officials personally handed him invitations, and both seemed genuine in their wishes that Iraq join the other teams. Actually, the exchange was quite cordial, with Termite telling them, "We'd love to come." Immediately

118

upon returning to Hilla, Termite issued the R.S.V.P. via e-mail that they would indeed be traveling to China.

Termite waited for confirmation and details of the tournament, but nothing came. Phoning the Chinese, they told him that they failed to receive the e-mail. Termite e-mailed the weights and names of the boxers again. Upon following up, the Chinese again said they failed to receive his e-mail. The coach, increasingly frustrated, e-mailed again, but now copied personnel in Baghdad. Again, the Chinese denied getting any documentation. Waking at 4:00 A.M. to allow for the time change, Termite called day after day in an attempt to negotiate the bureaucratic maze – to find just one person who could help them. A week into the process, the realization hit that this was no administrative jumble.

At some level, Iraq was being blocked from the tournament. Speculation ran on several tracks, but most in the coalition held to this one: the former Chinese business relationship with the Hussein government had dissipated with the American invasion. This was a small payback to the United States for the war. The other possibility tossed around was that Termite's stand against corruption in the first qualifier resulted in the rescinding of the invitation.

Whatever the scenario, Termite persisted. Finally, the Chinese acknowledged receipt of e-mail with their entry information. His sigh of relief was short-lived as he delved deeper into the correspondence and found that China had changed Iraq's entry requirements for the tournament. The Chinese informed Termite that the hand-delivered invitations were no longer valid because they lacked the official seal of the Chinese boxing federation. The Chinese "offered" to mail a brand new sealed invitation to Hilla. The coach demanded of the Chinese, "Does everybody else have to have a stamped invitation?" With no further explanation, he was told "No, only the Iraqis." Of course, having any document mailed to Hilla was ludicrous. If deliverable at all, it would take six weeks to get the invitation from China to Hilla. The coalition camp was definitely not on Fed Ex's route. Of course, the Chinese knew this, but continued with their terms.

The coach set his alarm practically every morning for the call to the Chinese Boxing Federation. Some days he complained; others, he just begged. On patient days, he appealed to decency, sportsmanship, and the Olympic spirit. On bolder days, Termite confronted them about their obvious attempt to keep them out. For six solid weeks, he pressed the issue. The effervescent, find a way, never give up coach had hit a seemingly impenetrable wall of Chinese stubbornness. Day after day, as he failed to maneuver the political situation, a frustrated resignation crept into the corners of his mind. He continued to pump his team up for the second qualifier, yet he knew that his options were practically exhausted. He had no plan to get them to China.

Security options were exhausted as well, as the February, 2004 tension turned into March turmoil. Incidents of suicide bombs and mortar attacks continued their rise at an alarming level. Security normally reserved for Termite and the team was redeployed to securing utility and construction work sites. Keeping the team and the coach safe was no longer a top priority. Getting to the gym from the coalition headquarters was a nail-biting daily adventure. The Suburbans equipped with shooters were used for other purposes; actually, the coach no longer had a ride to the gym at all.

Termite's most frequent transportation to practice was now Ah-Med, a trusted young interpreter for the coalition. So dilapidated was his car that the windows only had one position – down. Ah-Med only parked the car on an incline because it frequently needed to be pushed to get the engine to start. After getting a push start, the lean Iraqi would jump in and they were off to the gym. Unfortunately, the car's engine frequently stalled on the most dangerous streets of Hilla, and Ah-Med would climb under the hood and tinker with the engine while Termite waited in the car. The coach always offered his help, but neither wanted to draw more attention than necessary. Apologetic, Ah-Med would head down the road again, both in danger – Ah-Med for being *with* an American, Termite for being one.

The security contrast was so extreme. A month ago, he traveled at high speeds amidst a shell of armor. Now, at an intensely dangerous period, he was frequently stranded in the middle of an Iraqi roadway with the windows down, an easy target for the bad guys. The coach relied on his knowledge that, in his estimation, 90% of the Iraqis were warm, compassionate people – it was that 10% that kept the adrenalin pulsating through his veins.

The gym where his boxers lived, practiced, and slept was now completely unguarded. Upon first returning from the Philippines, 'round the clock protection was still in force for the team. As security priorities shifted, Iraqi policemen guarded the gym, replacing U.S. military. They were pulled for critical areas, leaving Termite and the team to fend for themselves. Training for this second competition, their training facility was wide open for attack – no police, no military, not even a pistol was in the building.

Still they practiced. Every morning, Termite arrived at the gym in whatever transportation he could muster. Village children surrounded the car as it pulled into the gym. Termite always had something for them – bottled water, T-Shirts, caps, whatever he could bring. The boxers ran, they worked the speed bag, they sparred – building upon their experiences in the Philippines. Well conditioned now, he focused intently on technique. After seeing the state of judging in the Philippines, his guys were going to have to be sharp enough to take some fighters out.

They celebrated their successes, dancing and chanting "Iraq is back!" Three times a day, the Iraqi women from the women's center delivered freshly prepared food for the men. Fern Holland's passionate vision of freedom and rights for women in Iraq was spreading throughout the country. The founder of this and other similar women's centers throughout Iraq, Fern Holland was an attorney from the tiny town of Bluejacket, Oklahoma. Young and petite, with a vibrant mane of blond hair, she relentlessly worked for the women of the country. A veteran of the Peace Corp, she was a huge believer in democracy. Regularly working eighteen hours a day, seven days a week, she longed for longer workdays. The women's center in Hilla was an amazing accomplishment. Equipped with computers, lecture hall, sewing machines, and a kitchen for the catering business, women learned invaluable skills to become more self-reliant. The lecture hall brought speakers with formerly controversial topics, such as the power of the vote. In addition to establishing the centers, Fern gathered evidence of human rights violations around the country and provided legal aid to women.

Fern's mission could not be slowed by cumbersome security detail. She had her own car and traveled with her Iraqi aide, Salwa Ali Ousmashi, throughout the villages spreading the news of the centers and speaking with women about democracy and freedom. She knew the perilous situation being a women's rights supporter put her in. She told a friend, "We stand out, and those who dislike us know precisely when we come to town." Her great love for the women of Iraq made it a danger worth taking. She e-mailed a friend, "If I die...know that I'm doing precisely what I want to be doing." Her strong sense of purpose was realized as she authored the women's rights section of the country's interim constitution.

Termite and Fern shared an important common denominator – a love for these people. Termite was tired of catching rides to the gym and was considering getting his own car like Fern had done. One early morning, as Fern was preparing to head out in her black sedan for her day's mission in Karbala, Termite caught up with her to ask her opinion about procuring a car. Fern's response made sense. She felt more secure without an obvious entourage, and the car provided greater maneuverability across the country for her cause. At the conclusion of their conversation, Fern paused and asked Termite, "I wonder which one of us is going to get it first?" The question startled him. "What do you mean?" He asked. Standing in the road of the compound, Fern looked directly in his eyes, "We both have such a passion for helping these people, which one of us will die first, if not both of us?" They were both taking big risks, Termite, broken down on the side of the road with Ah-Med; Fern, blonde hair slightly exposed under her head covering, driving across the countryside of Iraq. Fern closed the conversation with something she had said before, "Well, if we get killed, it's worth it." Then she handed him a commemorative medallion celebrating Iraq's new freedom.

Fern and Salwa left the compound for their day's work with an additional companion, Bob Zangas, who was to take photographs. Brand new to the Hilla compound, the publicist was nervously excited about his first venture outside the relatively secure walls. A likable man in his thirties, he often played the guitar in the rec room at night. Termite watched the group's car stir up the desert dust, and then proceeded on with his hectic day.

Evening arrived and every vehicle was accounted for in the compound, except Fern's. Tension heightened with every minute the black sedan failed to appear. The evening turned into light, and Mr. Gfoeller summoned everyone for a meeting. Fern, Salwa, and Bob were dead. Stopped at a checkpoint, men dressed as Iraqi policemen surrounded the car and unloaded their AK-47's into the occupants. The Oklahoman who had instilled in Iraqi women the thought that they mattered and were owed some basic human rights had been brutally silenced. Her faithful aide, Salwa, an Iraqi woman who risked her life every day even being seen with this bold American, died. And Bob, in his first trip outside the compound since his weeks in Hilla, perished. The determined light of freedom, this woman on a seemingly unstoppable mission, was extinguished.

The reality of losing Fern, Bob, and Salwa fell swiftly. Neighboring Iraqi women, who had such great reverence for the woman, brought dishes of food and condolences to the gates of the compound for the grief-stricken. A curtain of sadness enveloped the camp as military grief counselors arrived. Working their way through grief stations, counselors told them that they'd asked themselves who would be next. Mahawi

123

leaned into Termite, "It will be us, my dear. Your passion is going to get us killed." That concept was already planted in Termite's mind. He and Fern were high profile Americans who took chances every day in order to help the Iraqi's. He and Mahawi had gone without security in so many cases, shrugging and whispering *"Insha'Allah."* The bad guys had taken Fern out – how much longer would he last?

Losing Fern, Bob, and Salwa took the wind out of Termite. The stunning loss of his dear friends softened his determination to advance his team. His single-minded focus of bringing real sports, untainted by Hussein, back to the country was replaced by a state of mind best described as a daze. His days were usually so hectically packed that the thought of death didn't creep in.

Losing three friends in one day, however, placed death front and center in his mind. He did not want to further worry his family back in Texas about his security. Those e-mails were generally upbeat. Instead, he communicated to Suzy, his old friend who'd grown up in the shadows of his childhood home. "Suzy," a barrage of e-mails began, "If I don't make it out of here…" Messages for his son, daughter, wife, and parents ensued. This woman he'd not seen in years – who'd never even met his family - became the keeper of Termite's wishes for his wife and children in case of his demise. There was some peace in having those messages in good hands. His motivator to navigate through this fog of grief, however, was his deep love for his boys, his team. He also needed some help from home.

Calling the Chinese morning after morning, the team was no closer to getting into the games than they were a month ago. The man who routinely found joy in overcoming obstacles was emotionally drained. Dejected and needing a shoulder, he called home. "Sharla, we're not going to make it to China." Awaiting consolation, Termite instead heard a quick, unexpected thump from the phone dropping. "Tessa," she called, "Your dad's giving up." Twenty seconds of silence fell on the phone. "Daddy," Tessa announced, "You've always told us that you could find a way to do anything. Call us back when you've found your way. You have a team of men and an entire country depending on you." After a quick "We love you" from his wife, the phone went dead. They'd given up a father and a husband to the people of Iraq for almost a year – they were not willing to accept his defeat. That was it. He'd expected someone to listen to his complaints about the unfairness of the Chinese and, instead, had received a short, firm reprimand from his family. The kick in his green Iraqi sweat pants was exactly what he needed.

Termite set his alarm one last time for the Chinese officials. "Look," he told them, "I'm about to give interviews with CNN, HBO, and a whole bunch of other people. I'm going to tell all of them that China refuses to let these Iraqi fighters into the games. I'm going to tell them that China is stopping Olympic dreams from taking place. Then, I'm going to place a phone call to President Bush. I'm going to explain to him that China refuses to give this Iraqi boxing team even a chance, this team that has overcome every possible obstacle. I'm going to tell him that these fighters, who had to practice with machine guns aimed out of their gym windows, will not be allowed to compete in your tournament." After a pause, Termite heard from the Chinese, "No, no, this has just been a big misunderstanding. We want you to come; we'll make it possible." Within a half hour, a fax arrived in Baghdad confirming Iraq's participation in China. Termite was unsure whether the threat of negative publicity or getting the White House involved was the determining factor. Either way, his boxers were heading to China. Termite had no idea how to reach the White House – he was thankful his bluff had not been called on that one.

Travel had become increasingly dicey. Termite could not travel with his team – it placed the boxers and himself in even greater danger. The coach and Mahawi headed to the Green Zone in Baghdad to catch a military plane to Jordan. The team loaded a bus for the same location. Flights out of Baghdad were sparse due to the volatile situation, and Mahawi and Termite waited for their opportunity to board a plane. While waiting, they got word that three boxers were stopped at the Jordanian border. Termite had never questioned the validity of his fighters' passports; he just assumed they were legitimate. Truthfully, he was afraid to question any of their travel documents. According to the border officials, the passports of these three fighters were definitively phony. They refused to let them out of Iraq for the tournament, but kept the boxers' money. Three weight-classes would not have an Iraqi fighter – a huge blow to the team.

The stonewalling on the part of the Chinese placed the team in the country just in time for the opening ceremonies. Lacking the luxury of acclimating their bodies to the climate or time zone, they had just enough time to see their flag raised and begin fighting. The smallest man with the big man's punch, Najah stepped into the ring first.

It was a tradition started in the Philippines. Lacking any source for boxing robes in Iraq, Termite resorted to something he'd seen in his youth. Attaching Velcro to the points of Iraqi flags, his fighters were literally draped in patriotism. The team and the coaches often reflected in the symbolism. They carried such a burden on their young backs, these first athletes of the New Iraq. They'd witnessed so much in their lives, from the tyranny of Hussein to the arrival of blazing U.S. troops, to the fall of their dictator's statue. Their country needed them to be there – to show that Iraq was truly back to its former self – back to a time when athletes were free to fight, or swim, or run.

Najah wore the flag on his back proudly as he climbed between the ropes against the Sri Lankan fighter. Such a small man, he was nevertheless all muscle – "ripped" as an American would note. The heavy weights had trouble getting the flags around them; Najah was cradled in it. Termite lifted the flag from the boxer's back and handed it to Mahawi.

The two boxers touched gloves and the lopsided bout began. Termite learned a lesson in the Philippines: the only way they'd get a decision was to really hurt the other guys. Najah was just so quick that his opponent had few opportunities to hit him. The first round was such a rout, but Termite's confidence was tempered by the fact that Chowdry and his men were running this tournament as well. Between the first and second rounds, Termite's advice to Najah was, "Son, you're doing great, you're way ahead on points. Have some fun, but be careful." At the start of the second round, Najah cut the fighter's eye, not with a head butt, but with a jab. The blood spewed onto the canvas, and the fight was stopped. Najah had won. Najah's huge smile lit up the arena. He grabbed the flag from Muhawi, stretched it out, and walked around the ring holding his country's colors high above his head. The boy who had grown up playing in the office of his dad's boxing gym had won in international competition. Termite instinctively lifted Najah off the ground, and then the fighter and his mentor embraced for the longest time.

Termite, through Muhawi's explicit translations, prepped his next fighter for the ring. Saraka, the fighter who broke down emotionally in the ring in the Philippines after that horrible decision, was 118 pounds of sheer determination. Definitely one of Iraq's best, he had pushed himself in training even harder for this tournament. Very aggressive from the bell, he threw authoritative multiple combinations. He took command of the ring. Just over a minute in round one, Saraka threw a straight right hand that his Japanese opponent slipped. Intended for the boxer's face, it landed sharply on the fighter's right shoulder. Instantaneously, the boxer's right hand dropped, dangling near his waist. The left hand pulled up to hold the dislocated shoulder, and the fighter turned to head to his corner, crying out in pain. The ref immediately stepped in between the two fighters to prevent Saraka from doing any further damage. After examining the boxer, the ref announced Saraka as the victor. The man who pounded on the canvas in despair in the Philippines now cried out in joy. Termite and Mawahi rushed out to hug him. From the streets of Baghdad, Saraka had risen from dire poverty to win an Olympic bout in China. Just the fact that he was allowed to travel to China was staggering – it was an incredible monument to what sports can do for a man.

127

An obstacle quite different than poverty plagued Ali, the team's heavyweight. The medical personnel in China said simply, "You can't box like this," referring to his extremely high blood pressure. Termite scoured the arena for the Chinese doctor he'd met in the Philippines. Remembering Ali's medical history from that tournament, he cleared him. A sweet guy who had struggled to fill the boxing shoes of his brother's, this was his moment to represent his country. Ali's strengths were his relentless nature, huge heart, and ability to follow directions. All those traits paid off as Ali knocked out his opponent from Qatar out cold. As the ten-count wound down, he walked triumphantly over to his corner and just smiled proudly.

The next round of the tournament brought decisions against Najah and Saraka. Both terribly disappointed, they now knew the feeling of victory at this level. Ali, however, dropped his next opponent cold as well. Winning a bronze medal in the tournament, Iraq had an athlete on the podium. Adding to the amazing moment was the fact that Ali's brother, the former heavy-weight king of Iraq, was in the stands. The past month of training focused on technique had resulted in great success. The sluggish athletes who arrived at the gym five months ago had not only brought pride to their country, they were on the cusp of being an international boxing threat.

The respect the team gained in China was tempered by the fact that not one decision went to Iraq's corner. The fights they won were either due to opponents being knocked out or to injuries resulting in stoppages. Najah's second fight was a clear victory – the officials sided with the Korean. Termite erupted at the officials about the corruption in the games. Termite was certain as well of Saraka's second round victory. But he knew that without the opponent's blood streaking on the canvas he would not get the decision.

In China, the coach was approached with similar references about gifts to judges. "Go along with the system so you'll get some of those decisions," he was told. He absolutely refused to pay for decisions. His love of the sport would not allow it.

Throughout the tournament, Termite was aware of Chowdry's presence on a sofa in the arena, but the coach's narrow focus on his team pushed his existence to a far corner of his mind. Unfortunately, an incident involving his Iraqi coaches and high ranking members of the Iraqi Boxing Delegation brought the conflict between the two men back to the surface. Passing through the arena, Termite was completely taken aback by it. Iraqi coaches and high ranking members of the Iraqi Boxing Federation were lined up to have photographs taken with "The Dictator." This man who'd stolen bouts from them, who had basically threatened their "Crazy American" coach, was being treated like a celebrity. The doors of Termite's temper flew wide open. "What are you doing?" he yelled at one of the heads of the Iraqi Boxing Federation. "This man," he lifted his arm towards Chowdry, "is stealing opportunities from your country. You're over here having pictures made with him!" Only one in the group spoke even broken English, but they all knew by his tone and volume that he was livid.

Termite located Mahawi for assistance. "Tell them we're having a meeting right now," he emphasized. Crammed in Mahawi's hotel room were the coaches, members of the Iraqi Boxing Federation, Mahawi, and Termite. The coach railed. "Chowdry is stealing fights from your boys, these boys who have worked so hard to get here, and you're lined up, smiling ear to ear having pictures made with him? What are you thinking? He's stolen fights out from under Najah and Saraka, and you're over there being buddies with him? Hopes and dreams have been stolen by Chowdry and his men. Why in the world would you want to pose for pictures with a man who wants to keep your country back?" He waited for a response, any response. Finally, one official spoke up. After listening, Mahawi explained it to Termite. "Chowdry is an important man, a man of stature. By having their picture with him to take home and share, their friends will see the picture and they will have greater importance by being in the picture with them." Termite was still furious, but understood. Termite calmed down a bit as he thought of Americans lining up for photo ops with wrestlers and basically anyone in the public eye. He instructed to all of them "Just stay away from him,"

The China tournament was a definite turning point for the team. They proved they could win in the ring, even under a corrupt system. Momentum was on their side. Another month of preparation for the Pakistan games and their chances looked very positive for having a boxer qualify for the Olympics. They were confident fighters now – equipped with tools worthy of fighting world-class boxers.

Arriving back in Baghdad, Termite gave the team a few days off. Of course a holiday in volatile Baghdad could not be described as relaxation. They needed to see their families and to share all of the excitement of the trip. In the Green Zone, no rooms were available for Termite and Mahawi. They were assigned a cot in one of the tents behind the palace.

That night, Termite stretched out and planned his approach for the next tournament. The sports world had witnessed the transformation from the day in the soccer stadium where they just busted each other to a team with formidable skills. He just had to get one of them over the line to go to Athens. They would soon get back to their training center in Hilla for further refinement. Together, they would find a way.

10

You're On Your Own

Termite awoke early next to fifty other restless inhabitants crammed into a huge, sand-colored tent behind the palace in the Green Zone. The collective tossing and turning from the sounds of mortars, bombs, and gunfire made for a tough night. Looking out over the sea of twisted blankets atop twin aluminum beds, he had one thing occupying his mind: getting himself and his team back to Hilla to prepare for the last leg of the boxing qualifiers. The improvement his boxers exhibited in the tournament was staggering and rewarding, but mostly motivating. Rather than be exhausted from the trip in from China, he felt sheer exhilaration. Just one boxer was all he needed to get Iraq to Athens. They were a presence in China, and with the skill they displayed, there was a good possibility at least one boxer would make it.

Termite walked to the palace to phone Hilla. He wanted to catch the first convoy south so that he could make preparations for Pakistan before the arrival of his team. He reached one of the heads of security in Hilla. The words exploded in his head. "You can't come back to Hilla, Termite," the security officer stated emphatically. "Things are so hot here now, there's just no way that you can come back." Termite implored, "I've got to get back there. The gym is there; we can't train here in Baghdad. All my belongings are there." A long pause ensued. "Termite," he spelled out even more forcefully, "You're not coming back here. There's an uprising going on here in Hilla. It's far too dangerous for you to come back. This is an order- you're not coming back to Hilla."

The words came so fast and so hard that they were hard to absorb. Termite immediately began developing a contingency plan, "I've got to have some funds. I've got to keep

131

the team going. Transportation, hotels, living expenses for the guys…" The security head cut him off in mid-sentence. "What money? Termite, there's no more money. That money for the team is being used for security purposes now. If you want to keep the team going, you're on your own."

He headed down the path to the tent. The words reverberated in his head – "You're on your own." He stared at the canvas ceiling. He was on his own? What exactly would he do on his own? The team was running low on funds. He calculated that they had enough left for airline travel to Pakistan, but nothing for training expenses. If someone qualified in Pakistan, there would not be a dime left over to get them to Athens. All of their equipment was in Hilla, their facility that brought so much pride to the team. His personal belongings were there as well – his clothes, his computer, his pictures, everything was in Hilla.

For two days, the coach milled around the Green Zone in a state of disbelief. He hung out in the rec room, the theater, and ate in the restaurant. He talked to anyone who he thought might have even the slightest bit of influence about the unfairness of the situation. "Is this how it ends, then?" Termite questioned Mahawi. "After all the obstacles we've overcome beginning at the soccer field blocks from here – is this how it ends?" Mahawi just listened and tried his best to settle the restless coach. "My dear, you've done more than was ever expected. I think this probably is the end."

By day three, Termite was climbing the walls of the tent. The one thing they had on their side, Termite figured, was that almost all of the team and coaches were somewhere in Baghdad. "Mahawi," Termite said, "Call the coaches and have them get the boys together for practice. We're not stopping now."

Mahawi and Termite walked down the sidewalk of the Green Zone to the bus stop. The two-mile bus ride brought them about a half mile of the entrance to the Red Zone. From that point, the American and the Iraqi walked past the logged-jammed maze of checkpoints armed with U.S. soldiers in tanks and Humvees. Lines of Iraqi workers waited to be searched for work in the compound. Termite and Mahawi walked away from the safety of the military to a spot a hundred yards outside of the entrance. In one of the most dangerous spots in the world, they waited for a cab to take them to practice. Wide open in an area known for car bombs and shootings, Mahawi cautioned to Termite repeatedly, "You're going to get us killed, my dear!" Finally, Mahawi spotted a cab and hailed it. Piling into the back of the broken down orange and white taxi, Mahawi gave instructions to the driver, and they tore off across the streets of Baghdad to the gym. Twenty minutes later, they drove down a dirt road to a cinder block building.

It was great to see the team who were like family now to Termite. Even though they had only been separated for a matter of days, the uncertainty of the situation now made the meeting more meaningful. Termite explained some of the new circumstances, such as the necessity of practicing in Baghdad. He specifically omitted the detail about the team's pending financial crisis.

The boxers enthusiastically gave the coach a tour of the facility in which many of them had trained. Half of the floor was rock and sand; the other side was concrete. On the concrete side stood four posts imbedded in the concrete, forming a twelve foot square ring. From the posts were two sagging bare ropes. On the floor of the "ring" was solid concrete with not a shred of padding. Adjacent to that ring was a larger, but not regulation, ring with scraps of loose carpet over an exposed wooden floor. Three heavy bags hung on the rock and sand side of the room. No speed bags, no jump ropes, and no crazy bags – they were back to where they'd started. Nothing in Termite's long boxing history had prepared him for a concrete ring, but they used it. They had the best practice they could muster for day one and agreed to meet back the next day. After ending their session with their chant of "Iraq is Back!" Termite and Mahawi stood out in the closest main road to the gym and waited for a cab again to return to the safety of the CPA compound. After standing in line to get inside the gate, they sat on the covered wooden bleacher area and awaited a bus back to the palace. The afternoon practice brought the same routine of flagging down a cab in front of the compound, but the return home pushed the darkness factor; they had to be in the compound before dark.

The next day, Termite and Mahawi again boarded the bus and again left the safety of the Green Zone. They dodged cars on the street jam-packed with Iraqis and stood at the same spot to catch a cab. A half hour ticked away, and cab after cab passed right by the two men, often times glaring at them as they drove past. Gravely concerned for their safety at this point, they considered a retreat back in the Green Zone. Finally, a cabbie pulled in next to them. Climbing in, they each noticed a gun situated on the seat next to the driver. As Mahawi continued a discourse with the driver in Arabic, Termite had to wonder, "Was this a set-up? Why had all the other cabs failed to stop until this one?" His fears were allayed as the driver headed down the dirt road toward the cinder block gym.

Transportation by cab was clearly not a good idea, but there were simply no other options, so they continued meeting the team in that manner for several days. There was no doubt in their minds that many more days of that routine would result in a dead coach. Mark Clark agreed, and called the Iraq Olympic Committee for protection; they agreed to take on the responsibility. The committee would provide security to escort them to practice beginning the next day.

Termite and Mahawi made the familiar trek out of the Green Zone. They crossed the intersection and surveyed the area for the designated vehicle they were told to meet. It was unmistakable. Once brown and white in the 1970's, so much of the body was rust-damaged that it took on an orangey color. One Iraqi, equipped with an AK-47 hanging from his shoulders, exited the old Suburban and quickly escorted Termite into the back seat. There were three men: the driver, the shooter, and one in the back.

As soon as the back door of the 5-speed vehicle slammed shut, they took off across the city at a high speed, down narrow back roads. The driver, a middle aged thin man, drove incredibly fast, but it was his lack of focus on the road that unnerved Termite and Mahawi. Swiveling his shoulder to look at the men in the back seat, he continued to talk to Mahawi, leaving the vehicle to mosey in and out of lanes. Intersections were a nightmare, with most of the traffic lights broken. The driver barely slowed down; instead he just veered around honking cars, and then quickly pressed the accelerator back to the floor. From the back seat, Termite yelled out over the constant grinding of the gears, "I'm going to be really mad if I get killed today!" Mahawi translated for the group, and they all laughed at the white-faced coach. Finally, they reached the dirt road, and relief swept over the coach's face. It was a harrowing way to get to practice, but as soon as he saw his team, the danger slipped momentarily from his mind.

The three men remained as their security at practice, and then Termite and Mahawi piled back into the old Suburban for the same adventure to the compound. The afternoon practice brought the same situation. The men were there waiting for them outside the Green Zone. Termite gripped the ripped vinyl bench seats, tried to retain his consciousness through a haze of gas fumes, and held on as tightly as possible through a different route to the gym. He had no choice but to trust them to get him there safely, so he just held on.

The next morning, Termite awoke with a sense of trepidation about getting back into that Suburban. It was difficult to know who to trust in Iraq, but his only other choice was to not go to practice. He'd passed the decision about whether or not he would die for his team over a month ago. And, for all the sheer terror of the drive, they had delivered him safely back and forth on day one.

Termite and Mahawi began the ordeal again at 6:00 A.M. They got off the bus, walked past the Humvees and tanks at the entrance of the Green Zone, and returned to their spot for the old Suburban. There was no sign of them. Minutes rolled into a half hour. Any American standing still in the Red Zone unguarded for that length of time was in substantial peril.

For Termite, a high profile target coaching their Iraqi team, it was simply treacherous.

On Mahawi's recommendation, they stood back to back to more effectively watch for trouble. They openly discussed the real possibility that they were being set-up. In addition to the average bad guys in Iraq, Termite had made enemies in the boxing community by taking a firm control of the team. There was no doubt in his mind that a couple of those boxing officials would love to see him out of the picture. Another ten minutes passed, and the Suburban pulled into the intersection. Only two men were in the vehicle, however, and both were unarmed. Walking to the Suburban, Termite and Mahawi quickly tried to assess whether or not they should get in or run towards the gates of the CPA compound. Mawahi turned to Termite and said, "My dear, it's up to you." Termite drew a deep breath and responded, "Let's do it."

"Where's our shooter?" Mahawi asked the same driver from the previous day. "We don't know," he answered. "He didn't show up, and we don't know where he is." Termite and Mahawi sat stiffly on the torn bench seats. Grinding the gears, the driver sped off, taking a different route from yesterday. The familiar, powerful fumes hit the backseat quickly. The driver changed directions numerous times to avoid make-shift roadblocks – they seemed to know exactly where the bad guys would be. Tearing through villages at a dangerously high rate of speed, they finally arrived at the gym. The morning practice ended and the men nervously entered the Suburban again. The day's afternoon practice was equally harrowing, and the return home got them to the gates just before sundown.

Walking into the Red Zone the next day, Termite and Mahawi were nervous and apprehensive. A small sense of relief entered their minds when they noted that the Sububan was there waiting for them. The feeling vanished when they realized that only one man, the usual driver, was in the vehicle. Crossing the intersection, they again had to make a quick, yet vital decision. "This doesn't look good," Mahawi offered. Termite agreed, but the overwhelming motivation not to let the

136

team down overrode his common sense. "Where are the other men?" Mahawi asked. The driver revealed that he had no knowledge about the whereabouts of either of them. The grinding of the 5-speed transmission began again, and they departed on yet another route to the gym.

Due to the state of the gym floor, Termite had no choice but to run the team on a nearby soccer field. Termite's security detail was now a somewhat frail middle aged Iraqi driver who apparently did not even own a gun. Nevertheless, the driver stood next to the coach as the team ran in wide open spaces. If the circumstances had not been so perilous, it would have been comical. Termite had to wonder, "Who's protecting whom here?"

Their transportation was so erratic that they awoke not knowing what to expect. Termite and Mahawi left their tent, ate breakfast, and caught the bus to the edge of the Green Zone. When the bus stopped at their drop-off point, the covered area normally there had been hit by a missile overnight – what remained was a pile of wood splinters. They exited the Green Zone to meet the rusty Suburban, stood in their designated spot, and waited. For a half hour they waited, their nerves edgier with every passing minute. "Where was their driver?" they wondered. First, they'd lost their shooter, then the second man, and now the driver. They both agreed to head back to the Green Zone. Mahawi and Termite shared the same instinct that something just wasn't right. The next day was a repeat of the same. The men stood alone in the Red Zone, and no one came.

Termite expressed his frustration to Mark Clark in the Ministry of Youth Sports. The team had so much momentum just two weeks ago, but now they'd unraveled to the point that their own coach could not even get to a practice. The only hope for the team was to get them out of Baghdad. Mark was working on a better idea. He was trying to get them out of the country all together.

Again, they awoke in their tent with one thought on their minds: how to get to practice without getting killed. Their only option, and it was a very weak one, was to hope that the Suburban was there again.

At breakfast, something occurred that changed their course of action. Two Iraqi women, employed as workers in the palace, approached Mahawi at their table. Entirely cloaked in black with the exception of small openings for their eyes, they spoke quietly to Mahawi in Arabic. "Tell the American not to go out today. They are going to kill him. They have set up road blocks and will kill all Americans and any Iraqi with a CPA badge." The warning was astounding, both for its content and the messengers. Termite questioned Mahawi, "Do you think they're telling the truth?" Mahawi undoubtedly believed them and asked Termite, "What would they have to gain in telling us a lie?" They called the Iraqi coaches and told them to proceed with practice on their own.

The subsequent day, the women relayed to Mahawi the same message. "Tell the American not to go out today. They will kill him." Mahawi called the Iraqi's coaches' cell phone and told them to hold practice without Termite again. Termite was immensely grateful that the women had found the courage to warn them, in fact, he believed them to be angels out to protect him, but he had a team to worry about as well. How could they get to the Olympics if he couldn't travel twenty minutes from his tent? They needed to be back in a real training center where they could focus on boxing. That evening, Termite read an e-mail from Najah, stating, "Mr. Termite, don't come to the gym. It's too dangerous. It's not safe for you to come." Things looked bleak for the team. Their funds were dwindling, their coach was trapped in the compound, and their last chance to qualify for the Olympics was rapidly approaching.

Mark Clark had just the right answer at the perfect time. "Termite, Great Britain called and has extended an invitation for you and the team to train for Pakistan at the Crystal Palace. Termite...all expenses will be paid by Great Britain." Termite was obviously thrilled. Mark continued, "When do you want to go?" Termite grinned for the first time in days, "Right now!"

Preparations began immediately to get the team to Kuwait by bus for their flight to Great Britain.

In just one phone call, the team was back on track. As was always the case for this team, when circumstances were the most desperate, someone came through for them. Relieved from the news of the trip and happy that they would not have to stand in the Red Zone like deer at a gun show, Termite and Mahawi headed to the Saddam's former theater in the palace and watched a movie. That night in the tent, Termite scrawled notes on training and trip arrangements on his legal pad. "Training an Olympic team in Great Britain – life just can't get much better than that," he thought.

Having spent a year in Iraq at this point, Termite, like most everyone, learned to sleep with one ear open. Accustomed to gunfire during the nights in Hilla, in just a week in Baghdad he'd learned to recognize the sound of mortars leaving their cylinders. At 4:45 A.M., he heard just that familiar thud. Almost simultaneously, he heard "INCOMING!" shouted by someone outside the tent. A loud explosion rocked the tent. Termite and Mahawi's beds were positioned by the flap in the tent. The compression from the mortar knocked Termite out of his bed and onto the floor. He grabbed his pants and pulled them on hurriedly, as people began rushing to the exits of the tent, gripping their chemical weapons suits.

Mahawi watched the commotion calmly and then turned over in his bed. Termite yelled at Mahawi, "Get up! Get up! We've got to get to the palace!" Mahawi, looking bothered by the entire situation, told Termite, "My dear, if they're going to hit us, they're going to hit us anyway." Termite had been respectful of the Muslim philosophy of "Insha'Allah" up to this point, even used the word from time to time, but this was a moment for "save your butt," not wait and get killed. He stood over Mahawi and screamed over the sirens some words that were foreign to Termite, considering the tremendous respect he had for the man. "Mahawi, I'm *ordering* you to get out of that bed and evacuate to the palace." Mahawi reluctantly got out of his bed and followed Termite and the others to the palace for safety. As more incoming mortars sounded, the occupants of all the tents emptied quickly and filed downstairs to the shelter in the lower levels of the palace. After a half hour or so, silence replaced the sirens and people returned to their beds, shaken that they'd been rocked from their sleep in an area of the Green Zone seldom hit.

Termite was shaken too. He was obviously rattled by being blown out of his bed by mortars, but he was also unnerved by how quickly things had changed for the team. One week, they were winning fights in China; the next, he couldn't even get to them. They needed to get out of Iraq – quickly.

Throughout that day, explosions rocked the city, as smoke hovered on the edges of the Green Zone. An uncertain sleep that night ended again in the wee hours with the thud of mortars and the screaming of sirens. Again, the residents of Termite's and the other three tents behind the palace emptied into the downstairs bunkers.

Things were disintegrating in Baghdad, and they could not have picked a worse time to travel, but they had to get the team to Kuwait in order to get to Great Britain. The plan was to have Mahawi accompany the team into Kuwait on a bus; Termite would join them as soon as he could get on a plane. For obvious reasons, an American on the bus with the team for the long drive would have placed the team in grave danger. After a continued day of explosions and gunfire, the compound was again rocked from mortars during the morning hours. Termite, Mahawi, and the team proceeded with the only plan available. For six months, since the debut of the team in Hilla, the two men had been inseparable, and it was incredibly tough to say goodbye in these circumstances. They kissed on each cheek in Arabic tradition, and then bear hugged like two Texans. Mahawi left the Green Zone and caught a cab to meet the team and Iraqi coaches. The bus headed for Kuwait. Termite headed to the palace to get a military flight out of Baghdad.

He couldn't get out of Baghdad. Flights were suspended due to R.P.G. attacks, as were buses going to the airport.

Termite worried about the plight of his team on the road to Kuwait, but all he could do was sit in a holding pattern for days trying to get out of Baghdad. Staying in touch with Mahawi via cell phone, he was told the news: his boxers were stranded on the Kuwaiti border. For whatever reason, the person from the Kuwaiti Boxing Federation with the Visa letter never met them at the border. After waiting hours, the bus driver who transported them from Baghdad to Kuwait left them there. The boxers and Iraqi coaches had no place to go and no place to lay their heads. The border guards told them they could not stay there, but they had no transportation to go anywhere else. Their Kuwaiti contact person's phone continued to go unanswered. E-mails flashed across Iraq: "Extreme Urgency – Boxers Stranded at Kuwaiti Border." Problem solving with divergent ideas floated quickly over the Internet: "Send then back to Baghdad," "...definitely do NOT return to Baghdad." The waiting continued at the border, and the team finally located a hotel a half hour from the border. Every morning, they returned to the border and tried to cross into Kuwait, but they were refused.

Termite, unbearably frustrated at not being able to help his team, finally got a flight into Jordan, where he immediately hopped a flight to Kuwait. He located Ali Belushi, the former heavy weight king who played such a pivotal role in getting the team to the Philippines. The border patrol allowed Termite to visit his team. Stretched out in a large circle on the ground, the coach lifted their spirits and gave them one of his "we'll find a way" talks. The official problem with some of the team stemmed from wanting new CPA stamps for the boxers, but the unofficial reason for their refusal was their suspicion that Iraq's light heavyweight was a terrorist, and the changing climate in Iraq forced Kuwait to strengthen its border policy. The terrorism charge was ridiculous to Termite, who knew the boxer to be utterly sweet and non-threatening.

Three, four, five days went by. Occasionally, one boxer would get through the tough political filter at the border. Hours later, another fighter would be allowed to enter Kuwait. Then, for the longest time, no boxers or coaches came across at all. The team's airline tickets to Great Britain had already been delayed to a later date. In the e-mail to the Brits, Mark Clark stated, "...the arrival of the boxers will be delayed until we can sort out this mess." A decision had to be made about this "mess." Termite had no choice but to take the fighters he could to the airport and get to Great Britain while there was still a week and half of training time. He explained to the remaining five boxers and one coach stranded on the Iraq side of the border that they could still come if they could get across the border. Termite gave the tickets to Ali Belushi and left with the remainder of his team. They never made it.

Landing at Heathrow, the contrast in mood towards the team was striking. Hours before, they had been interrogated by border guards. Now, they were being interviewed by television stations and newspapers. The British media couldn't get enough of their story. "What was it like under Saddam? What's it like being coached by an American? What do you think of Great Britain?" Reporters marveled at their composure under pressure.

But Termite knew them. They were the most resilient athletes in the world. Western athletes talk about coming back from a sprained muscle. These men trained in the middle of a war zone. They stumbled over bombed out craters in the road to get to practice. They slept with mortars going over their rooftops and went to funerals for relatives killed in the war. He knew them because he'd lived with them for six months, and he was determined to see at least one of them in the Olympics.

11

Out of the Frying Pan

The hot pink dingle balls hopped up and down in front of the mirrored walls of the bus that carried the team to their lodging in Pakistan. The psychedelic splashes of colors, predominately neon orange and scarlet red, flashed against the drab Karachi highway. Positioned tightly in front and back of the Greyhound-sized bus were old army trucks with canopies flapping over their beds. Scanning the roadways were shooters poking out of the roofs of the two trucks, ready to use the attached fifty caliber weapons if anyone threatened the team. Nestled under the back canopies were six Pakistani soldiers with machine guns. Positioned on benches in the bed, their bodies swayed with every sharp turn the bus driver took. Resembling the Partridge Family touring in a war zone, their airport transportation was another reminder of the unique nature of the team and the coach.

The exhausted boxers sank into the plush, crushed-velvet seats and gazed out at the crowded streets. Entire families piled on single motorbikes dotted the highway. With Dad as the driver and Mom riding sidesaddle on the back, the two children rode wedged precariously between the handlebars and the driver's torso. Equally flamboyant busses, all with the cursory dingle balls jiggling above the drivers' heads, fought for lane domination, swerving in and out of the lines. Motorcycle families were pushed entirely off the road by the team's bus driver, only to pop back up behind the busses. Pleas from Termite to "Slow this bus down!" went unheeded as the bus weaved in and out of lanes at dangerous speeds.

The military protection that encased them was very late in coming. With Pakistan a known hot spot for Al-Qaeda cells, the plan was for the military to whisk the team off the plane from Great Britain and escort them to the hotel. Forced to move

143

from relative security in the airport building to a concrete pavilion outside, they team and coach waited for the military for over four stressful hours. A gathering of curiosity seekers assembled from seemingly thin air. The first half hour brought thirty or so men who were friendly in demeanor. The subsequent hour brought a larger and larger throng around the entire team, but most particularly their American coach. As the crowd pressed closer and closer to the coach, Termite felt himself being pulled away - divided from his team. His boxers instinctively circled closer to him. "It's O.K., Mr. Termite, we won't let anything happen to you," they reassured.

Tension escalated with each passing moment that the team stood stranded at the airport. By the third hour, the crescendo of pressing human flesh reached a peak as the throng of now hundreds of Pakistanis enveloped the team and coach. Most emptied into the airport from neighboring streets, wanting to see the foreign boxers arrive from the tournament. Some were airport workers who stopped to study the sight of the Iraqis and the lone American. Their massive presence made it difficult to move about at all, and Termite just gripped the handle of his garment bag and searched the roadway for their ride to the hotel.

Termite's brain recycled the caveat he'd received from numerous security personnel: "You're an American. While in Pakistan, stay inside." Trapped here outside the airport, it was an impossible order to follow. Heckling in Arabic commenced from a few in the crowd. More aggressive taunting followed. The level of concern in Mahawi's voice rose with each check of his watch. "My dear," he whispered, "Things are not looking so good. We cannot continue to remain here." Despite the confidence of the youthful fighters in protecting their coach, Termite and Mahawi both knew the reality of the situation: Karachi was a very dangerous city in the best of circumstances. Left much longer in this tough spot to fend for themselves, there was a real possibility that this crowd would get out of hand.

The military's tardy arrival was at least decisive and blatantly obvious. The bus and military vehicles swung sharply

144

in front of the pavilion. The wall of Pakistanis parted immediately, and two armed soldiers plucked Termite from the crowd and escorted him quickly to the bus. The team's luggage was stowed rapidly and they were finally off. The soldiers in the lead truck yelled in Arabic and motioned for people to "Get out of the way!" They stopped streams of dense traffic in approaching intersections for the team to pass. A presidential motorcade brought less of a ruckus.

The commotion of the procession ended in an abrupt halt at the hotel. The cognizance of the last opportunity, the final fights, was evident in the faces of the coaches and fighters as they climbed down the steps of the bus. The celebrity-status treatment they'd received in Great Britain was a reprieve from the war zone training of two weeks prior. Media followed them everywhere, from Buckingham Palace to their ride on the world's largest roller coaster. On the streets, they were warmly recognized and greeted with encouraging remarks. They posed for photographs with many British fans. Few of these Brits were even boxing fans; they just wanted to encourage these unique athletes to "Hang in there!" or assure them that, "We're with you!"

Working their way through metal detectors at the hotel, boxers and coaches from previous tournaments rushed to embrace the team. An integral part of the Asian sports community now, friends they'd made in the Philippines and China welcomed them back to this event. A smaller team due to the Kuwaiti border situation, it was a testament to the fortitude of the coach and team that they were even able to get out of Iraq again in the current raging violence of the country. The warmth of their international greeting in the lobby of the hotel came to a chilling stop.

Chowdry's son-in-law, Shakeel, approached Termite. "Why do you cause trouble?" he bitterly asked the coach. An agitated coach responded, "Well, I'm here for the boys and I'm looking out for them. You guys are looking out for yourselves." The official brusquely ended the conversation in a hateful tone, "You're going to hold Iraq back by going against the grain.

Don't cause any trouble here." Termite retorted. "Well, don't steal my fighters' fights. If they win, let them win; if they lose, let them lose. Just be fair. You do the right thing and I'll do the right thing." The official scowled at Termite and sharply warned again, "Don't start any trouble." The coach responded, "Do the right thing and I won't have to start any."

The preemptive rebuke did not set well with the coach. Termite had spent days at the Kuwaiti border and was forced to leave part of his team behind, an incredibly tough decision. He'd taken incredible risks to get to practices in remote sections of Baghdad. Their training warm-up in Great Britain had given his team a taste of what it felt like to be treated with respect, like the world-class athletes they'd become. Now in Pakistan, home base for the boxing corruption, the message arrived early that the team would not be given a fair shot. He hadn't even made it to his hotel room after the arduous situation at the Karachi airport, and he'd been admonished to accept business as usual at this tournament as well. This tournament was their last opportunity to get a fighter qualified for Athens, and it was in "The Dictator's" back yard.

He knew how far they would go to control the outcome of the tournament. In China, the corruption extended to the suspension of one of the Iraqi referees for not starting each round with a point for the Pakistani boxer. Termite knew that his fighters would probably have to drop their opponents in order to advance; he adamantly refused to provide "gifts" to the officials. Again, they would have to fight in the ring while their coach battled the system to get them the wins they deserved. It was incredibly frustrating that they had worked so hard for every shred of success and might be denied their chance in the Olympics because of a few unethical men.

After cleaning up from the day's travel, they headed together as a team to dinner. Najah said, "Mr. Termite, be careful what you eat. Pakistani food is very spicy." It was time to set the kid straight about Texans and their food. "Najah," Termite explained, "I'm from Texas. In Texas, we eat our food spicier than anyplace. I eat hot peppers and hot sauce for breakfast, lunch, and dinner. In fact, I can teach the Pakistanis something about eating spicy foods. There are no foods too spicy for me, Najah." The small boxer just shrugged and replied, "Ok, but I think you should be careful what you eat." Ravenous from the long day, Termite feasted on the Pakistani dinner.

The rumbling began about an hour and a half after dinner. Termite shot to his room and simultaneously had his head in the sink and his tail on the toilet. Periodically, he stumbled to the bed, only to return to the bathroom in minutes. Najah came in and out of his room and tormented him. "Oh, we're so tough in Texas. I eat spicy food for breakfast...nothing is too spicy for me," he mocked in his best Texas drawl. Termite so wanted to catch him, but just rolled his eyes and muttered back, "Very funny, Najah, I'm sitting here dying and you're coming in here torturing me." The boxer just continued, "I can show these Pakistanis all about spicy food: I'm one tough Texan." Mahawi chimed in, "You're definitely a hard-headed Texan, that's for sure."

By day two, Najah's humor continued, but with an underpinning of concern in his voice. Termite's bathroom vigil had continued throughout the night and dehydration had begun. He was so sick and weak that there was no possible way to be in the corner of the ring for the fights.

The boxers were summoned to his room. Termite explained that he was just too ill to be at the tournament today and that the Iraqi coaches would be there without him. They balked at the idea, not because they didn't respect the other coaches, but they were accustomed to his voice in the corner, his instructions, and relied on his motivational techniques. He understood as a boxer the psychological factor in making a change in the corner right before a fight. "Look," he explained, "You've got to do this without me. I'm not going to be here all of the time. These coaches have been with you all the way, too. They know what to do." The boxers tried to tell him, "We're going to win for you, coach," but he resisted those comments. "Remember," he told them, "You're not fighting for Termite

Watkins. You're fighting for your country and for yourself." He ended it with, "It's in your hands."

He exchanged kisses on the cheeks with each boxer and wished them the best in their bouts. He then spoke to the Iraqi coaches separately from the boxers. His job with the coaches for the past seven months was to teach current training methods to men who hadn't been out of the country for thirty years. It was hard to turn over the team at such a critical time, but he had to. "For the past seven months, this is what we've worked for. It's time for you to take over," Termite instructed.

In three days, Termite lost thirteen pounds. His condition just would not improve. Mahawi checked in on him frequently and gave him updates on the tournament, which was held about forty five minutes from the hotel. Najah ran into his room and announced "I won!" and gave him details of every round. Zuhair arrived later to tell him about his win in round one. Ali Taleb, a 64K replacement to the team, won as well. All the fights were decisions in which the Iraqi fighters just beat their opponents so convincingly that there was no wiggle room for the judges. As ill as he felt, he was also comforted in the knowledge that the boxers won with their Iraqi coaches. It was their team now, not his. The time was approaching where he would be out of the picture, out of Iraq. A competitive boxing program was now in place that would survive his departure.

On day four, Termite walked outside the hotel to the wildly painted dingle ball bus. He rode with his team for the last time to an Olympic trial. He proudly watched the Iraqi coaches in the corner of Zuhair's last fight; the boxer lost in a valiant effort. And he saw Ali Taleb, their new nineteen year-old they picked up late, lost in a highly questionable decision.

But the fight that caught his attention was in another ring. A Pakistani fighter was getting beaten so badly he was stunned that the referee had not stepped in to halt the brutal beating; in fact, the boxer never even received the benefit of a standing eight count. The Pakistani fighter was on the floor, after repeatedly being dropped by his opponent. His mouthpiece lay beside him. The referee picked up the boxer

148

and his mouthpiece and nudged him over to his corner at the bell. At the next bell, the boxer was literally pushed back into the ring by his corner man, forced to continue absorbing the pounding. His opponent knocked him down again, and the ref propped him back up to fight. In all of his years in the sport, Termite had never seen anything so brutal. The referee's job as the protector of the boxer was being ignored to get a Pakistani win at any cost, including the safety of the young boxer. This kid was being so viciously beaten that it was difficult for even the toughest boxer to watch, and no one would stop the fight. In the end, the boxer just refused to get back up off the mat, and the fight was finally called. It was horrible to see Pakistani officials force the boxer back into the ring for a continued beating. It was also difficult to watch other fights stopped for no reason except to guarantee wins for the favored teams.

The system was unfair to the boys, the coaches, and to the sport of boxing. Coaches wanted things to change, yet were caught in the system of providing gifts to get their boxers a chance in the ring. Chowdry's watchful presence in the upper level of the gym, surrounded by officials courting his favor, accentuated the depth of the corruption. The American's presence and vocal noncompliance in the wins-for-gifts scheme was a constant irritant for Chowdry and his son-in-law.

Time was closing in on Termite, the coaches, and the team. The last qualifier was over, and no one medaled, the standard for entry into the Olympics. Corruption in the Asian games played a part, but lack of time and inconsistent training conditions due to the war were a factor as well. Inevitability was in the sweaty air of the stifling arena – the inevitability that most of them would return to Iraq. To the concrete ring. To the cratered roadways. To obscurity.

All would return to Iraq except one. Termite disclosed to the boxers right before the Pakistan fights the Olympic decision that he had lobbied hard for. The International Olympic Committee had just awarded one spot for one fighter in Athens, regardless of their standings from the qualifiers. Termite, for months, had sold the vision of the team to officials at the IOC. In the beginning, he sold the concept of just lifting Iraq's suspension. As soon as that hurdle was cleared, he lobbied for an invitation for a boxer, just in case no one qualified. His message to them was not to punish athletes and average citizens for Hussein's sins. Termite reasoned, "Give the Iraqis some good guys to look up to instead of these bad guys they're accustomed to. They're going to follow someone, let's have them follow some good guys. By giving these boxers a chance, we're giving an entire nation a sense of what opportunity is about." Termite sent regular updates to James MacLeod about the progress of the team, telling him about their tremendous potential and incredible hearts. The coach had communicated since November of 2003 with the IOC, laying the groundwork for any possible scenario, win or lose.

Termite often reflected about the position he'd been placed in with the team. He'd relied on his sales and promotions experience as much as his boxing skills to get the team here. Comfortable with the media since he was an up and coming boxer, Termite had told their story in every medium every day for months. Sports enthusiasts in every country had seen photos of his barefooted men, had followed their progression and subsequent success. He knew that the telling of their story would benefit the team, the country of Iraq, and bring hope in dark days of the coalition efforts. There was another reason: worldwide support might sway the I.O.C.'s decision. It had to be a person skilled in boxing and sales to get the team here and he felt honored and humbled, but he also felt hand-picked, that it was God's plan for him. He didn't fully understand the plan, but he couldn't deny that it was more than coincidence that he was here.

The last full day of the tournament wound down, and the somewhat worn, slightly depressed team shuffled back to the dingle ball bus. The normally present military protection was no where in sight, but they were too tired to hardly notice. Fighters, individually and in groups, came to Termite and expressed through Mahawi their deep feelings of disappointment. Specifically, they felt that they had let him down. Over and over, the coach reassured them that they had not let anyone down; they were all winners.

Finally, he spoke to the whole team on the bus as they waited for their driver. "Look," he said, "I'm the happiest coach around. Hey, we've accomplished a great deal. We set a goal to get to the Philippines and we did. We set a goal to go to China and we did. We did the same thing in Pakistan. You are the first team of the new Iraq. People tried to hold us back from going to these places, but they didn't. You are all winners. I love each of you. And I admire every one of you for what you've gone through to get to this point." Whenever they were down, Termite returned to what he knew always brought them together. Looking around the bus, it began, "Iraq...is back! Iraq is back! Iraq...is back! Iraq is back!" Their spirits lifted somewhat, they settled into their soft seats as fatigue rolled over them. For some, exhaustion turned to giddiness. Zuhair and Najah were cutting up, laughing uproariously. Others had their heads laid back, already drifting into sleep. Everyone was ready for the missing driver to appear so they could get back to their hotel.

The doors of the bus opened, but not to the driver. Two men, both in their late twenties and dressed in traditional robes, boarded the bus. "Are you the American?" one demanded of Termite in very broken English. Termite, seated next to Mahawi and in front of his entire team, was uncertain how to respond. Not one to deny his American heritage, but concerned for the safety of all on the bus, he replied, "I'm the Iraqi boxing coach." Dissatisfied with his answer, the man asked again, "Are you the American?" Again, Termite gave the same answer. "I'm the Iraqi boxing coach." Moving in to within two feet of Termite's face, the same man announced, "Saddam Hussein a good man. Saddam Hussein a good Muslim."

Termite had told his team so many times over the past six months that there comes a time when a man has to take a stand. In his year in Iraq, he'd found the Iraqi people to be so loving that they had difficulty standing their ground at times. As the leader of the team, Termite felt compelled to take that stand

151

now, especially after the brutal treatment athletes received under Hussein's son. He rose from his seat and spoke emphatically, but calmly to the men, "Don't come on *this* bus talking about Saddam Hussein being a good Muslim. Saddam Hussein is not a good Muslim. Saddam is lower than a donkey. Good Muslims don't kill innocent men and women, innocent boys and girls, and innocent babies."

It happened so fast that Termite had not absorbed the potential danger they were in. The other Pakistani spoke for the first time. "Bin Laden good Muslim. He builds mosques for the people." Termite made eye contact, an easy task with their close proximity. "Bin Laden is lower than a snake's belly." The same man continued, "Do you know many Muslims?" Termite answered, "I know hundreds, maybe thousands. I've eaten with their sheiks and men in their villages. And none of them kill innocent boys and girls."

A moment passed with no further words, Termite standing in front of his team, the Pakistanis glaring at him, unsure what to think of this incredibly bold American. The one who spoke first stormed off the bus; the other lingered. He searched for the English words, "You're right, good Muslims don't kill *innocent* people." He exited the bus to join his friend. Termite immediately turned to Mahawi, "Have I just gotten us killed?" he implored. Mahawi responded, "My dear, quite possibly you have this time." Termite turned to his team, who had speculated that the men were Al-Qaeda. "I'm sorry about that, guys. Mahawi, should we leave the bus? Mahawi replied, "Don't say you're sorry, my dear, we should have been the ones who stood up." Debating about whether or not they should exit the bus and head indoors, the bus driver arrived and quickly cranked up the engine. It was time to get out of Pakistan.

Flying back to Kuwait, Termite knew what lay ahead of him. He had to say goodbye to the team of men he'd trained and grown to love so deeply. He also had to say goodbye to Mahawi Shibley, his closest friend and advisor. Mr. Gfoeller's wise judgment in handing over one of his top men to Termite and the team was fundamental to their success. They were an unlikely team, Mahawi and Termite. Mahawi, highly educated with his British accent, knew nothing about boxing in the beginning. Termite, with his Texas drawl and difficulty with verb conjugation, knew everything about boxing but little about Middle Eastern ways. What they had in common brought them together – they loved these boxers and were both driven towards achieving goals. In the corner, Termite's directions to his boxers were quickly translated into Arabic with the same intensity and gesticulation. They had become one for the team; two men who would do anything for these fighters. And they would do anything for each other. Termite loved and respected his dear friend. Telling Mahawi goodbye would be one of the hardest things he'd ever done, because he knew with the current situation in Iraq, Termite would probably never see him again.

The team spent just one night in Kuwait; the next day they would return to Iraq. Their bus was set to depart at 5:00 A.M., so the coaches woke them early for their last team meeting. Crammed into Termite's room, the coach addressed them. All the boxers were packed for the bus, but they all knew that one boxer would stay behind with Termite to begin the final training for Athens.

Termite looked at their faces for the last time. Tears of anticipation were already in the eyes of the few of the fighters as well as their American coach. He began his farewell address, "It has been such a privilege, an honor, to come over here and work with you guys. You have changed my life, and my life will never be the same. It's so hard for me to say goodbye, because this is probably the last time we will ever see other. I'm so very proud of all of you, what you've come through, and the obstacles you've overcome. Remember this, we found a way, and you can always find a way to accomplish anything you want, just like we've found a way as a team. Pass what you've learned to the guys who will come behind you."

Termite looked at the three Iraqi coaches. He recalled his shock in some of their first practices when the Iraqi coaches would smack the boxers in the back of their heads when they did anything incorrectly. Correcting them immediately, he

153

cautioned, "Never treat anyone on *my* team with anything but respect." It never happened again; in fact, they'd adjusted quite well to Western-style motivation. He told them, "I was supposed to be teaching you, but I have learned so much about life just being with you. I know that it has been hard for you to stand behind an American, an American who came over and replaced you in your position, but you've handled it so well." The coaches hugged and thanked him, saying that it had been an honor working with him.

The moment had come to announce the lone boxer who would represent their country in Athens. Situated on beds, coaches, chairs, and the floor, they listened intently to their coach. Fighting back his tears, he began, "Guys, we have a unanimous decision. The criteria we based our selection on were: attitude, work ethic, and best performance in competition. This decision came about by a vote of all of your coaches, not just me. Every coach received one vote. The boxer who has best met all of these criteria is Najah Ali."

Najah, who was sitting cross-legged with his back against the wall, responded immediately to the news. His head fell into his hands and tears of joy rushed down his cheeks. The team's tiniest boxer, the man who rushed up to the coach on the soccer field and declared that he would be "The One," would indeed go to Athens. Most of the team rushed to Najah and flooded him with congratulations. Two did not. Zuhair and Saraka, two of the most experienced fighters, were visibly shaken. Both headed immediately to the bus, sobbing over their lost opportunity. The room gradually emptied of boxers, leaving Najah as a team of one.

The time had come for Mahawi and Termite to say their goodbyes. Termite held both of his friend's hands, "Mahawi, I could have never done this without you. I want you to know that I'll always love you and I'll always be grateful. I'll never forget you, Mahawi." Mahawi, crying as much as Termite, said, "My dear, who would have ever thought we'd have ended up here? It's been a wonderful journey. We've come a long way together. You, my dear, have done a lot for the country of

Iraq. You are the one who got boxing back in Iraq. You'll forever be known as the father of boxing in Iraq." Termite reached out and kissed Mahawi on both cheeks, and then Mahawi grabbed his American friend and hugged him for the last time.

Najah and Termite walked to the bus together. His boxers had their hands outstretched from the bus windows towards their coach. Termite walked from the front to the back of the bus, touching all their hands one last time. A few were inconsolable, their journey over. All the athletes' eyes locked in on their coach as the bus pulled away. Najah and Termite watched the bus disappear towards the Iraqi border.

Termite put his arm around Najah, and they walked solemnly back to the hotel. Quietly sitting in his coach's room, Termite told him, "Najah, we've got to talk." Termite had debated in his mind whether to tell him or not. He decided to just be honest. "Son, the good news is we're going to the Olympics. The bad news is that we don't have any money. I don't know what we're going to do. I'm not even sure I can even pay the bill for this hotel." Najah smiled his soon-to-be-famous-smile, "That's O.K., Mr. Termite, we will find a way." It was a poignant moment, the young athlete pumping up the coach.

Najah didn't know all of the facts; however, Termite was already spending his own money, and he was not in a financial position to continue funding this expensive venture. For two days, the two men twisted in the desert wind of Kuwait, with no place to go, no place to train, and few funds left in Termite's dwindling bank account. They were unaware that wheels of hope were turning on the other side of the world.

12

Ambassadors of Freedom

The wet June heat in downtown Atlanta was miserable for the German and Japanese athletes, yet comfortable for the boxer from Iraq. Termite stood only 5'8" inches tall, yet he towered over his athlete, who measured just shy of five feet. On the steps of the Marriott Marquis, the coach leaned into Najah and spoke deliberately, "Iraqi athletes have the biggest hearts in the world, Najah. *You* have the biggest heart of any boxer I've ever known. You *deserve* to be here, Najah. You're here representing your country, your people. Make them proud of you, because," He paused, "Iraq...is back! Iraq is back!" The chant was much quieter now with just two people, but Termite wanted to keep the chant alive so that Najah felt the continuity in his training regimen.

Najah took off running around the city block surrounding the hotel, weaving in and out of business people rushing to neighboring high rises. At his current 113 pounds, he was overweight. Termite had to get his weight down for the beginning of the Titan Games, a June, 2004 warm-up for the Olympics. Najah had quickly developed a love for American food, and had been sneaking ice cream, M &M's, and French fries. Seven pounds was substantial for a boxer his size, and Termite now had the painful job of working it off of the fighter. Dressed in bright orange nylon sweats, the hungry boxer ran endless circles around the Marriott. As he passed the steps signaling a lap, his coach hollered out, "I'm hurting you 'cause I love you, Najah!" and jotted down his running time. It was only 10:00 A.M., and this was Najah's second run this morning. The first was before the sun was up, and he ran him around the circle of rooms in the open designed lobby. Najah wasn't the only fighter running against the scale. German and Japanese fighters were running on different floors from the Iraqi, dodging hotel maids with their carts. Weigh- in was in two days, and he would not fight unless he came in at or under 106. Termite would not allow that to happen; he wasn't going to bring this kid half-way around the world and have him sit out.

How they got halfway around the world was another example of people extending their hands at the most critical times. Stranded in Kuwait, the two men could not return to Iraq and lacked the funds to go anywhere else. A country's sole hope for Olympic boxing and his coach sat in a hotel room, a room Termite could not continue to provide for financially much longer. They prayed, at times separately, at times together. Termite kept telling Najah, "God is never early or late, he's always just on time." Termite believed in God's timing, but he had to admit that God sure was cutting it close.

Finally, two rescue calls came in. The first call was a tremendous relief; the second an answer to a prayer. John Epstein, founder of Playing for Peace, had heard about the predicament this unusual team was in and offered some much needed financial relief. That help solved immediate pressing problems – room and board, for one. The second call was unexpected and profoundly pivotal. Don Whittle with the U.S. Olympic Committee asked this one question, "How would you and Najah like to come to the United States and train?" It was beyond anything Termite or Najah had even fathomed.

The sequence of events that led to this offer was either amazingly coincidental or a perfect example of divine intervention. Germany had accepted an invitation to the Titan Games in Atlanta, but their106 pound fighter had dropped out of the competition. There was one vacant slot for a 106-pound boxer, and, of course, Iraq's only boxer was in that weight class. Germany offered the slot to Najah. If Termite and the Iraqi coaches had selected any other boxer, the offer would have never materialized. As thoughts of coming home with his boxer raced through his head, the next question from Don came, "Would Najah like to train with the U.S. Olympic boxing team?" Najah, an Iraqi boxer, would fight on Germany's roster in Atlanta and train with the U.S. Olympic Team. That so many international wheels had been turning to help this boxer and coach was historic, even in Olympic proportions.

Just the thought of taking one of his boxers to the states was exhilarating to Termite; it was particularly meaningful because it was Najah. From the moment the young fighter rushed up to him on the Baghdad soccer field, Termite felt something special for him. A talented athlete, what really separated him from the pack was that he always did what was asked of him, no matter how difficult or painful – he was a coach's dream. As a person, his genuine, loving nature drew people to him, and his impeccable character, cultivated by his parental upbringing, deepened Termite's respect for him every day.

Najah reminded Termite of himself as a young boxer. The size comparison was obvious, but the will to succeed and intrinsic motivation to constantly better himself struck a chord with the coach. Najah's connection to his father touched Termite, and reminded him of the sacrifices Bill had made in Termite's career. Over the nine months they'd been together, the regard between the two men strengthened. In short, Termite loved him like his own son.

When the ballots of the coaches were tallied for the one boxer from Iraq, Termite felt such a joyous relief that Najah had garnered three of the four ballots. He cared deeply for the entire team, but he was certain that this was the man that most deserved to go. It was a small lesson in democracy, and it worked effectively. At one point, the Iraqi coaches, hesitant about this voting idea, wanted Termite to make the decision (and take the consequences) alone, but he refused. They had to vote; to do things fairly. Now Najah would be the one to go to the U.S., to train with one of the best boxing teams in the world. What thrilled the coach the most was that he was bringing Najah home.

Termite and Najah first touched U.S. soil in Chicago for a quick layover before a media blitz in New York City. Dressed in his usual jeans and T-Shirt, his short, jet-black hair maintained its typically meticulous style. Najah could have been any young man heading to any unknown destination, but he was *the* Iraqi boxer sent to train with the team whose country had invaded his own nation. The fighter's warm, magnificent smile that generally occupied his face was slightly subdued from twenty years of anti-American indoctrination. He was a bit jittery about what Americans would think of him and how he would be treated.

Flagging the first cab, the cabbie grabbed their luggage, and then looked up at Termite and Najah. "You're that boxer! You're that coach!" Excitement covered his face as he reached out and robustly bear hugged Najah, and then Termite. "Thank you so much for what you're doing!" he exclaimed. Settling into the back of the cab, Najah whispered to Termite, "Are all Americans this nice?" Najah asked Termite. His coach broke it to him, "No, unfortunately they're not, we have our bad ones too, just like Iraq and every other country."

Descending into New York, Najah was mesmerized by the skyscrapers. Whisked into a waiting limousine, the two men went from one media event to another. *Time Magazine, Sports Illustrated for Kids, Good Morning America, The New York Times* – this engaging, genuine Iraqi won over the most cynical of reporters. Najah accepted what they asked and answered with tremendous composure and honesty. Armed with intelligence, boyish charm, and dignity, Najah fielded politically sensitive questions better than any programmed congressman. He was the voice of the average Iraqi, and Americans craved real information about his country, something other than the graphic images flooding their television screens. Questions about the horrible treatment of athletes in Iraq came at every stop. Najah explained to Americans what it was like to worry about returning to Iraq from a boxing tournament if an athlete had not performed well. Questions about the American coach. "He's like my father; I love him." Questions about politics and the American invasion. "Without our freedom, I could not have come to America or go to the Olympics." This sole Iraqi boxer had a fascinating story, and everyone wanted to hear it.

Najah worked out at the world-renowned Gleason's gym, while camera crews captured every punch and rope skip. As reporters and bystanders learned about him, Najah was soaking up American culture. A female boxer at the gym, much larger and tougher-looking than Najah, brushed by him. "She scares me," he said, grinning at Termite. A nearby reporter overheard and laughed. The boxer was so accustomed to traditional female roles in Iraq– women's boxing was a lot to take in on day two in America for the kid from Baghdad.

For most who heard him, he was much more than a boxer. At a time of a huge military operation with casualties racking up daily, Americans reflected on the words of this refreshing ray of hope, a wholesome Iraqi athlete who thanked an entire nation for helping his country. Just the obvious love between coach and athlete was a reminder to everyone that people can find areas of common agreement. Americans had seen so many media interpretations of Iraqis, usually extremists with swords drawn or firing guns into the air. Here was a real Iraqi, and he was a sweetie. He didn't have his face covered in a black mask and he wasn't preparing to execute some innocent aid workers. Najah was a recent college grad who just wanted to box in the Olympics. He was just like the neighbor's kid, the grandson, or the kid down the hall in the dorm. Najah put a face on the Iraq that the United States was trying so desperately to help. He was an Iraqi citizen worth dying for.

The New York trip put Najah and Termite's faces on major news organizations across the U.S. The Houston trip gave Najah a real taste of life in America. Arriving at the airport, three local news cameras focused on their faces as the two men descended the escalator. The hometown boxing hero turned Olympic coach put his arm around Najah's shoulder. "Welcome to Texas, Najah."

A crowd of Watkins' family and friends stood at the base of the escalator. Most had spoken with Najah over the past months and could not wait to get their arms around him. It was a homecoming for both of them. Najah and Termite had been a family of sorts on the road for the past months. Now it was time for Najah to be welcomed into an American family.

The scenery on the forty-minute drive from the airport to Deer Park held Najah's complete attention. The massive freeway spaghetti bowls amazed him, but instinctively both he and Termite instinctively glanced upwards for enemy fire. Closing into the Deer Park area, most observers would hone in on the refinery flasks and vast holding tanks along the Houston Ship Channel. Not Najah. Having grown up in a dirt road desert village with homes connected to one another, the boxer found the bright green grass in all the yards fascinatingly beautiful. The roads and driveways were so neatly organized – he'd never seen so much concrete.

Pulling into the driveway of the three bedroom ranch home, Termite was anxious to get Najah settled in, but as they opened the door, the young boxer froze in his tracks. The man who never flinched as bombs were pounding his home was terrified of something he'd never seen inside a home – dogs. Sugar, an aging Bijon and Blazer, a frisky black lab inadvertently held the Iraqi motionless. As the rest of the family dragged luggage across the threshold, Najah's feet were firmly planted on the porch. "Come on in, Najah." Termite invited. "No, no, I'm afraid of them," Najah whispered, pointing at the two dogs. Najah didn't know what to think. In Iraq, dogs frequented the villages as protection, but were not domesticated and were often carriers of diseases. After coaxing Najah inside, the dogs gave him a sniff and settled in. Najah was shocked at the way Americans treated dogs almost like people. Within a day or so, however, the dogs were curled up at the foot of his bed.

Najah's quickest adaptation came with the big screen television. Accustomed to only two channels in Iraq, the Watkins willingly relinquished control of the remote, which remained in Najah's firm grip for most of the trip. It was tough to watch television with Najah, because the channels changed constantly; he went up and down the channel selection over and over, rarely stopping for more than a moment. Reruns of every sitcom from the 50's onward mesmerized him. So much to see, so little time.

After a few days of rest and raiding the fridge, Najah and his coach hit the gym. They pulled up to the metal building on the edge of the channel, the Galena Park Boxing Academy. As soon as he entered Kenny Weldon's gym, everyone rushed to shake his hand. As Najah unpacked his gear from his athletic bag, his expressive dark eyes glanced up at the huge posters on the wall. There was Termite's teenaged beaming face looking down at him. It was taken the year his coach won the National Golden Gloves Championship. Clippings of Evander Holyfield dotted the wall, along with other champions. The worn, chipped tape on the floor showed the scores of boxers who had found their rhythm here. The upper cut, crazy bags, and speed bags, the ring – this was where his coach, his mentor, had fine-tuned his skills as a boxer. Najah wanted to know everything about western boxing that he could glean, and he was in exactly the right place.

Najah stepped into the ring that so many amateur and pro champs had learned the ropes in. Kenny Weldon climbed the short ladder up to the side. So did Bill Watkins, a changed, sweetheart-of-a man who had left alcohol behind so many years ago. Termite climbed in with the mitts to drill his boxer. "Termite, he needs to keep his hands up. He's dropping them just like you used to." Termite responded, "Dad, he can get by with it." Bill continued, "Well, you know how I am son, I like to see those hands up." "Termite," Kenny chimed in, "He needs to get his weight on his back foot." Termite nodded and repeated the instructions to his boxer. Kenny traded places with Termite in the ring for further refinement with the boxer, and Termite moved next to his father and critically observed his fighter. Here, Najah was not an oddity. No one here expected him to give a treatise on complex problems in the Middle East. He was a boxer training for the tournament of his career, and they were going to do everything they could to make it happen for him. The circle was complete. The men who had worked so hard to make Termite successful were leaning against the ropes offering advice to this young boxer. As young girls and teenage boys worked the circuit around the ring, a hundred years of boxing experience poured into Najah.

Najah needed to process that information as efficiently as possible, because there were only two months left before Athens. There was no doubt that he had talent. One day in the gym, Kenny pulled Termite aside and said, "Man, this kid can punch, Termite. He punches like a heavyweight." In fact, Najah reminded Kenny of Termite. "He works hard and he listens, just like you did," Kenny added. Time was their only enemy now, but it was a formidable one. Najah had faced so few styles of boxing in the ring; he needed to see as much as possible for the next eight weeks.

A hundred and thirty-five pounds of style arrived at the gym to spar with Najah. Louis Woods, a professional featherweight with tremendous skills, climbed into the ring with him. Louis completely controlled the Iraqi, and frustrated Najah at every turn. So skilled and so quick, Najah could not catch him, even when Louis was right in front of him. Older, bigger, faster, and much more experienced, Najah was totally outclassed on day one. But the next day and every day after, an improved Najah sparred against Louis. Training in Houston marked a turning point for Najah the boxer. Staying in Houston opened his eyes to America.

Whether driving through Whataburger with Termite, running at the high school, or just hanging around the house, Najah loved America. In the same way that Termite embraced Iraq's customs, Najah opened his mind to American ways. Mid-trip, something happened in Deer Park that would have never taken place in Iraq. Amber, a teenaged friend of the Watkins' pulled into their driveway to take Najah out site-seeing for the day. They toured the San Jacinto Monument, the Battleship of Texas, and just hung around the mall. While they "hung out," Termite paced like an expectant father. In Iraq, Najah would never date a girl even casually without approaching the father of the girl first. In fact, until he reached the university, he never

163

even went to school with girls. Termite knew this wasn't exactly a date; he was just nervous enough about the possibilities and wanted to see Najah walk through the door. Around 10:00 P.M., Najah walked in beaming and talking about his great day. His American dad relaxed.

One aspect of American culture Najah was especially curious about was religion; he wanted to understand what Americans believed in. A devout Muslim, he obviously had no plans for conversion, but Najah had an insatiable curiosity about everything American, including "church." They drove into one of the older parts of Houston, and situated across from George Foreman's health clinic and community gym was the boxer's church.

Najah and Termite entered the sanctuary after the service had already begun, and George Foreman's face erupted into a grin. "Well, I see that my buddy's back," he said, referring to Termite. Najah and Termite squeezed into a pew and Najah listened intently to the lesson. After the service, George wrapped his huge arms around Najah's shoulders. "I'm so proud of you for what you've accomplished, Najah," George told him. He wished the boxer luck in the Olympics and they visited for a time. George rarely allowed cameras in the church to maintain the focus on God and not him; however, this was one of those rare occasions. "Who's got a camera?" George asked the crowd, and one soon emerged. From his small village in Baghdad, this boxer found himself posing with this great American sports legend –his life was a swirl of incredible events.

It was time to leave Houston and head for the Olympic training camp in Michigan, and ambivalence was the mood. Najah was excited about training with the U.S. team, but he was so comfortable in Houston. Their itinerary dictated that they fly back to Chicago to connect with the U.S. boxing team, and then proceed with them to Michigan. As Termite and Najah walked through the terminal at O'Hare, the red, white, and blue Olympic uniform backs were easy to spot. Termite and Najah, both with their typical broad smiles, approached the boxers.

"Hey, guys," Termite asked the obvious questions, "Are you the USA boxers?" They looked up at Termite blankly and nodded dully. "This is Najah Ali; he'll be training with you." The total vacuum of enthusiasm persisted. One fighter nonchalantly glanced up from his seat. "Where's he from?" he blandly inquired. "Iraq," Termite answered. "Oh," the boxer replied, and then turned back to his team. The decidedly blasé reception was deflating for Najah, who missed the team he'd left behind weeks ago. Termite was slightly perturbed, but chose not to reveal that to his boxer. "Najah," he comforted off to the side, "You've got to realize that they don't know you yet. They'll come around." In reality, Termite wasn't sure that they would. These were street-wise, cool kids who showed not even a hint of empathy for this boxer who had traveled around the world to train with them, to learn from them. "This could be a long eight weeks," Termite reflected, as the two men boarded the plane for a mostly silent trip to Marquette, Michigan.

In the dorm rooms at the Olympic Training Center, all the boxers settled in with roommates in rooms that were adjoined by bathrooms. Najah, instead, roomed with his coach. At the sound of the alarm clock at 6:00, Termite woke him for his first day of training with the team. They joined the team downstairs for stretching in a circle before the morning run. For Termite, it was like dropping a kindergartner off for the first day of school. He wanted to protect Najah, but he had to let him go, to let the other coaches and boxers work with him as well. Najah awkwardly lay back behind the circle, not quite sure what to do. Finally, Devin Vargas, the U.S. heavyweight, rescued him. "Come on, Najah," he invited, "If you're going to be part of us, you need to get in here." The two-hundred-pounder reached for the little Iraqi and pulled him into the circle. Termite wanted to hug Vargas.

Every day the walls of indifference came down, brick by brick. Najah's tremendous work ethic impressed every boxer and coach. The morning runs were dominated by Najah and Andre Ward, the two fastest men on the team. Punch by punch, Najah proved himself to them. In the first days, Ron Siler, his

165

training partner, worked quietly next to the Iraqi, probably regretting the partner pairings. Every day, however, things loosened up. Termite started hearing the two motivating and pushing each other, "Come on, Najah!" he'd encourage. One evening in the common area of the dorm, Devin Vargas started messing with Najah, pushing him around in a playful manner. With a weight difference of a hundred pounds, Najah went up to Devin, poked him in the chest, and kidded, "I'll take care of you later!" Termite knew at that point that Najah was starting to fit in. When Najah came downstairs with his baseball cap flipped backwards and headphones on, the coach quit worrying.

The Titan Games in Atlanta presented a great opportunity for Najah and the other athletes to compete against Olympic athletes they might face in Athens. It was a gauge of sorts, a warm-up to evaluate the athletes' current performance level so that training could be tweaked in time for Athens. The Titan Games brought boxers, weight lifters, wrestlers, fencers, and other athletes in the "toughest" of sports together in a few venues across Atlanta. It was a mixture of sports and entertainment, with high-energy pulsating music and a meandering announcer calling out highlights as they appeared on huge screened television monitors.

In the middle of the throbbing energy of the Titan games, Najah was the main event. His early morning runs around downtown and late nights in the room with Termite were the athlete's only solace from media events. There were so many media requests for time that Termite found himself in a quandary. He needed his boxer to be focused and rested, but he also needed to prepare Najah for the pressure of the thousands of media who would be present in Athens. There was another issue: Najah's story was uplifting at a time of so much bad news coming out of Iraq; it was important for people to hear it. And they did. The primary question every reporter asked: "What do you think of America?" It was as if Americans needed to hear from an Iraqi citizen that this military engagement was worthwhile. Najah explained that growing up in Iraq, he'd always heard that Americans were evil. "But Americans," he assured, "Are wonderful. I love America. When Termite came to Iraq, he learned that most Iraqi's are good people. Then I came to America and learned how nice Americans are." His workout at Atlanta's Art of Boxing was on the local sports, their pictures were splashed across the sports section, and as the two men ate in the restaurant hotel, their voices sounded on the evening news.

Termite decided that he would shield Najah from the media until after his first fight, but a call from CNN requesting a live interview changed his mind. CNN had covered the team from the first practice in Hilla, and this was a great opportunity to tell a world-wide audience about Najah's place in the Olympics. They were beat, but they hopped into a cab and raced a few blocks over toward the CNN building. Entering the maze of security to get into the station, they saw groups of people huddled around television monitors. The images flashed of the breaking news: insurgents had beheaded an American in Iraq. Najah was visibly shaken. Termite told CNN something they'd already figured out on their own – this was not the day to interview an Iraqi athlete.

Termite shuffled his boxer into a cab and headed for the hotel. Just an hour prior, a photographer had spent an hour posing Najah proudly draped in an Iraq flag with the skyline of Atlanta in the background. Undeniably proud of his heritage, Najah was sickened by some of the horrific actions taking place in his country. Termite tried to comfort him, but knew that few words could help at this moment. "Najah, it's going to be O.K. We have to move forward, Najah. Every day you're showing the world what most Iraqi's are like. Whether you wanted to be in this position or not, you're a representative of your country. You're it, Najah, just continue doing what you're doing. You know how some of the media have been calling you and I ambassadors of freedom? Well, now it's time for us to be that, Najah. Tomorrow you box. Walk out proudly in the ring with the flag of your country on your back and show the world what Iraqis are really like."

The next evening, Termite and Najah boarded the charter bus carrying the German team for a venue a half-hour from downtown. Officially on the German roster, Najah's first fight was with a Mexican boxer. Termite had asked the U.S. Olympic coach, Basheer Abdullah, to join him in the corner for Najah. As with all fights, Termite extending his arms. "Let's have a word of prayer," Termite instructed, and the three men held hands. Termite prayed for a hedge of protection around both fighters, for guidance, and that both fighters would perform to the best of their abilities. Basheer, a Muslim, then read a prayer in Arabic.

Najah's entered the ring draped in his country's flag. Television cameramen stood on the edge of the ring, recording his every move – even a Middle Eastern news agency was ringside, broadcasting the fight in Arabic. Termite lifted the Iraqi flag off of his boxer's shoulders and kissed him on each cheek. The canvas that night was a United Nations of sorts, with an Iraqi boxer fighting for Germany, a Muslim U.S. Olympic coach, an American Iraqi coach, and a Mexican fighter who had to wonder what all the hoopla was about.

Evander Holyfield and Vernon Forrest settled into their seats, but more importantly, the entire U.S. Boxing Team sat ringside next to Najah's corner. The Mexican fighter stood in his corner, unnoticed by everyone except his coach. Najah came out looking quick and strong, but the Mexican fighter soon adjusted to the Iraqi's game. By round three, the Mexican fighter threw Najah's rhythm off kilter. Fighting the Mexican style of boxing, the Mexican fighter was right in Najah's face, a style Najah had not seen before in the Eastern games. By round four, it was a slug fest, which was exactly what the Mexican fighter wanted. A burst of enthusiasm boosted Najah from ringside, as his new American buddies, the entire U.S. Boxing team, stood and rooted him on, and loudly. He was now a part of their team, this unlikely addition, and they offered their full support and ringside advice.

Saddened by the loss, and sure that he had won, Termite quickly straightened him out, "Najah, you didn't win this fight.

I'm always going to be honest with you about your performance. You failed to follow the game plan. You let your opponent control the fight. We've got some things we've got to work on. We failed tonight, but without failure, there can be no success. We're now one step closer to success. We have to move forward now, Najah and correct the mistakes I saw tonight. This is where we correct mistakes, not in Athens."

Termite and Najah opted to skip the bus ride back downtown, and rode back with Suzy, Termite's reclaimed childhood friend who lived in Atlanta. Crammed in the back of a Mitsubishi Eclipse with her two teenagers, Najah watched the driver miss exit after exit. Najah studied the disappearing downtown skyline as they traveled down I-285. Scrunched against the armrest in the backseat, Najah's warm voice asked innocently, "Suzy, how long have you lived in Atlanta?" Feeling a bit sorry for the cute Iraqi who'd just lost a fight, the driver responded, "Sixteen years, Najah, why?" Najah grinned, "Because I've only been driving for a few years, and I know every street in Baghdad." The driver did what she would have done to any backseat driver, foreign or domestic. She turned around and teasingly slapped his leg. "That's for telling me how to drive, Najah." Everyone in the car burst out in laughter. Najah learned a lesson in dealing with American women – they're sensitive about their driving.

Armed with the knowledge of what had to be accomplished before Athens, Termite and Najah headed for the Olympic Training Center in Colorado Springs. Pulling up to the vast facility adorned with Olympic rings, Termite felt such pride in his boxer and himself. From the small Hilla gym guarded by machine guns, this had been quite a journey. One of the most advanced training camps in the world, this was the place where Termite had trained as a young boxer. Now, Najah would reap the benefits given to world class athletes in this most critical phase of his training. One month before the opening ceremonies, and Najah would spend it here getting his game ready for the world.

Seeing Najah fight against Western competition lit a fire in Termite, who in turn ignited Najah. "I'm going to hurt you because I love you, Najah," his coach warned. Every time Najah heard that, he knew he was about to feel the pain. The training intensified. He ran faster and trained harder. Termite worked with Najah on executing a game plan regardless of strategies employed by his opponent to divert that plan. Sparring against two of the world's best amateurs, Ron Siler and Rasheed Warren, Najah's skill level elevated on a daily basis. He needed to fight above his level, something he'd never done in the Middle East, in order to be competitive.

Termite pushed him almost beyond his physical and mental limits. In fact, Termite began questioning himself at that point. He knew that he was hurting Najah. Termite also realized that this was a once-in-a lifetime opportunity for the fighter. Termite had lived for thirty years with burning midnight questions of his missed opportunity in the big fight. Whatever happened, he wanted Najah to leave the Olympics comfortable in the knowledge that he'd done his best. It was also critical to the coach that he left this Olympic venture with the certainty that he'd given this extraordinary athlete all he could in preparing him.

Najah rose to the challenge. Of course, he really only had two options: get to the next level fast or get his tail whipped. Everything kicked in. In sparring, Najah was no longer the foreign boxer being offered advice; he was now on equal footing in the ring. Even though all the U.S. boxers cared deeply for Najah, sparring sessions now got heated and highly competitive, with punches continuing even after the bell. They were now good friends, but in the ring the friendship ended at the ropes. Training with these great American athletes pushed Najah to the brink of his potential; Najah was so formidable in the ring now that anyone who stepped on the canvas with him had to bring their best game to beat him – he was an Iraqi on a mission. One of the U.S. members told the media, "We just pray to God that we don't draw each other on the first night." Najah had earned their respect as an athlete as well as a person.

Najah was at his peak performance, and the U.S. coaches and Termite could not have been more thrilled with his fantastic progress at the camp. Two weeks before their departure for Athens, Termite was pumped – what he'd been saying from day one, that Najah had a chance of medaling, was coming to fruition. This kid from Baghdad was going toe to toe with the best Americans; he might just stun the world.

Unfortunately, a peak can be a slippery thing. It's there one day and then can fall to a quick descent the next. It had come on slowly over days, but something was wrong with Najah. Termite was having the toughest time getting his dynamo out of bed in the morning. Normally a quick starter, Najah began begging Termite for extra time to sleep. After roadwork and breakfast, Najah climbed back under the covers for most of the day until afternoon training. When he wasn't training, he was sleeping. In sparring, Najah started strong, but then faded quickly. Termite examined his training log for clues – had he overworked the boxer to the point of exhaustion? .

Najah had hit a wall. Actually, a wall hit him, but it took about a week of valuable training time to sort it out. The wall was his new American diet. Najah's insatiable appetite and love of American food drew him into the cafeteria; in fact, he was eating more than the heavyweights. Najah's weight was right on target now due to the strenuous training, so his coach had ceased watching his intake. It wasn't the amount that was tiring him so, but the type. Filling up on ice cream, white bread, potatoes, and rice, the kid was on a processed carbohydrate binge. He had moments of high energy, followed by hours of dead sleep. After just two months of living an All-American lifestyle, Najah had become an Iraqi couch potato. Termite had to turn the all-starch all-the-time ship around in a hurry or risk having a lethargic boxer in Athens. Strict supervision of lean meats, vegetables, and fruits were imposed, and every time Najah entered the cafeteria, Termite was hot on his trail, measuring portion sizes and keeping a log of his intake. Najah was back on pace and becoming more mentally prepared every day. His lifelong spiritual preparation continued quietly as well, as he unrolled his small rug and prayed five times a day in the privacy of his room. Having spent ten months with the devoutly religious boxer, Termite was worried that Najah had not been to a mosque in the past couple of months due to their travel schedule. His coach was cognizant of the role his own Christian needs had played in making him a complete athlete and man. Termite sought Basheer's assistance.

Najah and Termite accompanied Basheer to a local mosque for a service presented in Arabic and English. Taking their shoes off at the entrance, they were greeted by the Muslims with handshakes, a kiss on each cheek, and open arms. The men, and there were only men in the mosque, sat cross-legged on the floor. The cleric delivered the daily lesson of loving thy neighbor, a theme Termite had heard many times in his own church. Of course, the prayers were quite different, but the atmosphere was as warm as any church Termite had ever visited. Najah glowed with comfort, practicing his religion and sharing this important part of his life with the coach he so loved.

It was time. Najah had fallen in love with everything American, the superficial entertaining things like infomercials and I Love Lucy re-runs, Mexican food, and backyard swimming pools. But what moved him was the freedom in every day life, something Americans have taken for granted for two hundred years. Najah could speak about Saddam Hussein here, a suicidal act across the ocean. In fact, he could say anything he wanted. He visited churches and learned about different ways that Americans worship. He went to a mall with a young woman totally unescorted. He experienced the pain of being driven around Atlanta by a woman born without an internal compass. And he pursued excellence in a sport without any concerns about what might happen to him if he had an off day in the ring. Najah loved America, and America opened its arms to this tiny Iraqi boxer, the same way that America had welcomed millions of others before him. This love of freedom now burned in Najah, and he was ready and determined to go home and spread the news of what he had learned.

13

The Perfect Fight

Olympic credentials dangling from his neck, Termite climbed farther and farther up the stairs of the stadium to find a seat. Squeezing through the row of spectators' knees, apologizing, "Excuse me, excuse me," he found a seat. He looked down over the thousands of people in front of him, and focused in on the field. The Opening Ceremonies were magnificent, but he just wanted to see one thing – Najah enter the arena. Finally, the world's athletes began their procession. Blocks of colors were all that Termite could see from his altitude, so he relied on the huge television screens posted throughout the arena. He waited for his athlete's appearance.

Country after country streamed in, usually with large teams, and they waved their flags and their hands at the crowd and worldwide audience. About midway through the procession, the country of Iraq was announced, and a small block of green began rounding the field. The crowd's roar reached a quick crescendo in appreciation of Iraq's small team, and then one by one, the stadium stood in an ovation to the athletes who had endured so much for their sports. The soccer team consisted of the bulk of the team, with a sprinkling of other sports. And there was Najah, the country's only Olympic boxer, waving his pint-sized Iraqi flag. Najah's smile woke up the world, as he beamed gloriously at the crowd and the cameras. Najah's eyes searched the crowd for his mentor, but it was impossible with the thousands and thousands of people. He strode proudly in his green and white Olympic suit around the perimeter of the field, and then settled in with his team in the center of the field next to the other athletes.

Termite's face streamed with tears. So much more emotional now than he was when he started this journey, he made no effort to force a retreat of the tears. He announced to the group of strangers seated near him, "That's him, that's my boxer. He's worked so hard to get here. If you only knew what we've been through to get him here." People nodded and smiled, not quite certain of the proper response in this situation. Termite's cell phone rang. "Termite, can you see me?" Najah's warm voice questioned. Of course, the coach could see little of the activities on the field from his distance. "Yes, Najah, I can see you," he fibbed. "How do I look, Termite?" Najah asked. Termite told the absolute truth, "You look wonderful, son." Najah paused for a second and said, "Termite, thank you. None of this would have happened without you." The coach strained to conceal the flowing tears from Najah, "You're welcome, son." Najah continued, "Termite, you should be with me down here." Termite answered him in the only way that would make sense, "This is your time, not mine, Najah. I want you to enjoy every minute of it." Najah asked the question that was really on his mind, "Termite, are you O.K.?" Termite reassured him, "I'm fantastic, Najah."

Termite was not fantastic a few hours prior to the ceremony. He'd been in such a media frenzy on behalf of Najah that he hadn't even stopped long enough to wonder why he had not received his uniform for the procession yet. An Iraqi Olympic official pulled Termite aside after an interview and asked to speak with him. He explained to the coach that his presence next to the Iraqi athletes would increase their danger of attack when they returned to Iraq. "It's your decision, Termite, but we know that you would not want to endanger Najah's or any other athlete's life."

For ten months, he had incessantly pursued this goal, the team's goal. From the opening minutes in Hilla, the boxers' dream of seeing their flag fly in the Olympics was expressed. As the team whittled down to one, Termite and Najah talked late into the nights about walking into the Olympic stadium holding hands, something they had never been able to do on the streets of Iraq. They wanted to show the world how two people from warring nations could love one another. That dream dissipated with the words of the official.

174

At first Termite fought it, saying that he would be at Najah's side no matter what. Of course, he deferred to the concerns of the Iraqis, but it was a heart-breaking decision. Thoughts bounced around his head – was this just politics? Did someone at some level make the decision that Termite's presence in the procession would send the wrong message to the world about America's presence in Iraq? In the end, his decision had nothing to do with Iraq or politics. Termite anguished about what he considered the real issue – would his presence, so dominant in the media, overshadow his boxer? He decided in the end that it was Najah's turn to soak up the spotlight, not his. He had done his job – he'd gotten an Iraqi boxer to the Olympics, and now he had to begin stepping aside.

It hurt. Najah was hurt as well, and was determined that his coach walk into the Opening Ceremonies with him. "Termite, if you don't go, I won't go either. We started this out together. You're the reason I'm here, and if you're not going, I'm just not going," Najah insisted. Termite sat him down and explained, "Najah, you don't understand, you have to go. This is your country, and this is your time. You've got to go represent your country. I'll be fine." Najah reluctantly and tearfully agreed." It was one of the biggest decisions of the American's lifetime, and it left him as a spectator on the sidelines - the only coach who didn't walk in with his team.

That disappointment aside, when the ceremonies ended, Termite and Najah focused singularly on winning the first fight. The Olympic Village was an incredibly vibrant place where athletes from every corner of the world lived side by side. Several square miles of new dorms were encased with razor wire-topped walls, but those daunting walls were dismissed from their minds as they moved freely within their own safe little town. It was a "Green Zone" of sorts, with military patrols guarding the perimeters, but the inside was one huge welcome mat. Banners and flags of the different countries hung proudly from third story dormitory rooftops. Busses ran in constant circles, dropping athletes off at swimming pools, the outdoor theater, or the multi-acre international restaurant.

175

Tucked inside the dorm with the Iraqi flag and banner, the sole American resided with the Iraqi team. Every distraction beckoned to Najah. Knocks on the door brought invitations for fun, inside and outside the village, from soccer players and wrestlers. The first few requests Najah brought to Termite for a response, but after hearing, "Najah, after the fights," several times, the boxer quit asking. Termite made every attempt to keep blinders on his athlete, to maintain the intense focus Najah had developed while training in the United States.

The media presence was so intense that they could have occupied every moment just on interviews, but the coach managed that as well. Termite picked up his media requests in a bin every day and sorted through them. He and Najah gave a multitude of interviews; of course, the same questions had been asked a hundred times before. For Termite, "What's it like working with the Iraqis?" To Najah: "What's it like having an American coach?" What the world failed to understand was that they had not seen each other in those terms for almost a year. They were simply a boxer and a coach, two human beings, who saw each other more as father and son. Najah expressed his gratitude for the United States and his intense patriotism for his own country, "Representing my country, especially now with a free Iraq, I consider this the best thing in my life." Termite and Najah appeared on television screens in living rooms around the world with a sincere message of, "Yes, people can get along, even Iraqis and Americans." As they were smiling and charming the media, both were focused on one thing: the first fight. Najah had to win.

Winning would prove a challenge, because they had both seen his opponent, Kwak Hyok of North Korea, fight in the Asian games. A head and a half taller than Najah, the coach knew that this guy could beat the Najah of ten months ago. However, the new and improved Najah, fresh from two months of training in the U.S., posed a much bigger threat. The edge Najah had recently cultivated came about the painful way of getting in the ring with much tougher, more talented, opposition.

Basheer once referred to Najah as a "good student." That student had studied hard in the United States. He had learned how to box against different styles and how to follow a well-devised plan, rather than to just depend on instinct and past training.

His last week of final preparation in Athens consisted of roadwork around the Olympic Village and afternoon sessions in a curtained-off gym that allowed privacy for each boxer. Najah was at a great weight, maintained by six small, healthy meals and three weigh-ins every day. Termite knew where every ounce of weight was on his diminutive boxer and watched every sip of water and morsel of food that he consumed. Focused and peaking at the right time, Najah's gym work was all refinement and sharpening of skills. Termite concentrated on pinpoint jabs that could rack up points. All of their practice at this stage was in the ring, with Termite as the opponent. Mitts on his hands, Termite forced Najah to come after him, to turn him, and to force him in the center of the ring. Kwak was bigger and stronger than Najah, and Termite did not want his boxer against the ropes with that disadvantage. Over and over, Najah threw combinations and hit precise jabs to the head, the chest, and the body of his coach. The game plan was enacted repeatedly and exactly: hands up, chin down, and turn your opponent to keep him in the center of the ring. Strategy, finesse, and precision were Najah's boxing strengths; his huge heart and will to win for his country were the immeasurable elements that completed him as a fierce competitor.

The closer the fight moved towards them, the more relaxed Najah became. He kicked back in his dorm room and visited with other Iraqi athletes. Termite and Najah took walks around the village and watched movies at the outdoor theater. They ran into boxers they'd met around the world, including the U.S. team. Najah and Termite stopped and posed for pictures with athletes and coaches who had heard their story in the media. Najah just enjoyed this time. Termite's response to the pending fight was quite different. Always loose in the ring as a boxer, he was in a nervous knot about Najah's fight. While Najah slept soundly, Termite paced the small area of the dorm room. The mental checklist of last minute preparations ran without end. More important to Termite than his national Golden Gloves title or Las Vegas title fight, Najah's biggest fight was his as well. Najah needed to fight the perfect fight to win. Termite knew it, and his boxer knew it.

The fighter had that youthful indestructible confidence, but his seasoned coach had the hard-earned knowledge of two hundred fights that kept him awake at night wondering if he had prepared him for every possible situation in the ring.

After a restless night of blanket wrestling, Termite waited for the time to awaken his fighter for the 8:00 A.M. weigh-in. Najah was thirsty from drying out the day before, with no liquids or food after 6:00 P.M., a typical routine for a fighter. Termite sat next to his boxer on the bus, with a bottle of water, Pedialyte, and bananas for Najah's consumption immediately after he stepped off the scale. "105 pounds," the official called out. A little lighter than he wanted him, they were both relieved that he'd made weight.

Walking away from the scale, a dreaded voice from the past bellowed out, "He can't fight. His book is not up to date." Termite and Najah turned and saw Shakeel, the son-in-law of "The Dictator," the powerful boxing head of the Asian region. "The biggest day in Najah's life is not going to be stolen here in Athens," Termite vowed silently. This was Greece, not Pakistan. Termite looked at Najah's medical booklet, which is handed to officials every time an amateur steps into the ring. "The missing entry is from one of your tournaments," Termite blasted. "If it's not updated, blame *your* people, not Najah." Shakeel reiterated, "Najah can't fight tonight."

This attempt to rob Najah again was like a head butt reopening a bad cut from the Asian tournaments. Their time in the U.S. had pushed the memories of the Asian corruption to the far corners of the coach's memory, and he was mentally unprepared to fight Chowdry's gang in Athens. Termite's boxer instincts for self-protection kicked in, but the sensations that spread from his brain to his fists were for Najah. This coach who had been blown out of bed by mortars and had hitched rides with armed Iraqi strangers to practice in a war zone had taken enough. Termite's eyes took on a steely determination. "He will fight today," Termite warned, "Or I will kick your butt right here." Shocked Olympic coaches, officials, and athletes were stunned into silence as the confrontation escalated into a boisterous nose-to-nose shouting match. U.S. coaches watched in bewilderment, unaware of the past battles Termite had fought against corruption at the Pakistani's hands. Even though they weren't sure what the problem was, they jumped in to help Termite and Najah. As Termite cocked his fists, a U.S. coach offered a possible solution, "Termite, see if that American doctor will sign him off." Termite and Najah presented the booklet to the doctor and explained the situation. He quickly signed his name. Returning to Shakeel with the document updated, the Pakistani grabbed it out of Termite's hand in disgust. Najah would fight.

Seeing his coach almost get into a fight at weigh-in wasn't the calmest start for a fight day, but then nothing about this team had been normal from the coach's machine- gunned introduction in Baghdad. The rest of the day went as planned - walks around the village, small meals, and visualization of the game plan that had been drilled into Najah's head. Termite never left his side for the entire day, keeping him totally focused on the fight.

It was the fight of his life, the first fight of the New Iraq. Every goal they'd set, every obstacle they'd overcome was for these eight minutes, these four rounds of two minutes each. Termite again had asked Basheer to be his corner man; the United States had done so much for Najah that it was important that the U.S. coach be there. The three men were seated in a private pre-fight room. They prayed, Termite went first, Basheer followed in Arabic.

Walking through the hallway to the packed arena, Termite and Basheer sandwiched the shadowboxing fighter between them, not allowing the swarm of media to distract the boxer. Termite promised them, "He'll talk to you guys after the fight." Najah entered the ring to thunderous applause from the crowd. His red shirt displayed the team's motto, Iraq is Back, first in Arabic and then in English. (Olympic rules dictated that

179

Najah could not wear his Iraqi flag into the ring, and all boxers wore either red or blue.) The announcement was simple, but everyone in the crowd had at least some knowledge of the complexities of getting this Iraqi fighter to this ring. "From the country of Iraq, Najah Ali." The crowd rose to their feet in a booming standing ovation.

Najah went to his corner for his final instructions. Termite, dressed in green shorts and a white shirt that stated boldly on the back "IRAQ," looked into Najah's eyes. "Najah, keep him in the center of the ring. Out point him, jab to the head, jab to the body, jab to the head, right hand to the body. Don't throw any hooks, all straight punches." Termite kissed him on each cheek. "I love you, son." The fighter replied, "I love you, too." Najah smiled and reassured his nervous coach, "We'll be O.K." Termite had to smile at the composure of this man with an entire country on his shoulders.

He was so much better than O.K. Everything he'd learned in Hilla, Iraq; Galena Park, Texas; and Colorado Springs, Colorado flew from his fists. Jabs to the head, right hands to the body. When he got tied up, he threw his hands out and his chin down to avoid any holding calls, a weakness that had cost Najah point deductions in the Titan Games. He stuck to the plan perfectly. He kept his head moving so that he was never a target, he moved in and out, side to side. Najah took the North Korean completely out of his rhythm. At the first round bell, Najah led in points, 9-3.

In the corner, Termite asked him simply, "Najah, are you having fun?" The boxer nodded. "You're doing great, Najah," Termite always kept the instructions simple, understanding that in the middle of a fight, a boxer needed to hear it straight. "Jab to the body, jab to the head. Fake to the body, go to the head." As Basheer gave Najah his short sip of water, Termite reminded Najah, "I love you, son." Najah nodded, and Termite kissed him from cheek to cheek.

The second round was a great round for Najah. He extended his point lead to15-5, and executed their game plan precisely. In fact, one of the announcers calling the fight said, "What you've just got to like about Najah Ali is that he has a definite fight plan and he's sticking to it." In the corner, Termite told him, "Great round, Najah. Son, how do you feel?" Najah shook his head up and down, motioning that he was great. His coach continued, "He's got to come get you, son. Use hard jabs to the body and head." Najah's eyes started wandering to the crowd; he wanted to see all the people who had been so vocally rooting him on for the first two rounds. Termite had to redirect him. "Look in my eyes, Najah, and listen. I want you to throw all straight shots. Have a little fun now, son." Najah nodded at the fun part, something that he rarely had when fighting under the fear of Uday Hussein.

Round three brought a bigger 19-6 lead, and Termite knew the fight was Najah's. In the corner before the fourth round, Najah listened, "Son just move around, it's yours," Termite said, "I'm so proud of you, Najah." His boxer's eyes started looking around at the crowd again. "Look at me Najah, and listen to me closely. He's got to have this round big. He needs a knock out. Play it smart, keep your rhythm." Najah looked into his coach's eyes, and the moment was his. Najah's serious game face was gone, and his huge smile beamed from Iraq's corner.

As Najah touched the North Korean's gloves for the last time, Termite turned to Basheer and asked tentatively, "There's no way they can take this fight from him, is there?" Basheer assured him, "There's no way anyone can take this fight from Najah." In the ring, Najah was having a blast. He darted quickly around Kwak, dropped his hands and made the North Korean miss him completely. One of the announcers pronounced, "This is not just nervous energy, this is by design." The tiny Iraqi boxer put on a boxing show. As the clock wound down, the announcer noted that, "It had to have helped being at the U.S. camp boxing with Rasheed Warren, who was defeated earlier today." At the final bell, Najah went to corner, took off his gloves and head gear, and returned to the center for the lifting of the winner's hand.

As the crowd's voices softened to near silence, the announcement came, "From the country of Iraq, Najah Ali!" His hand was lifted high by the referee. Najah pointed his index finger to the rooftop of the arena. He pranced around the ring, shaking his finger in a "number one" sign. As the announcer said the words, "He fought the perfect fight." Najah was swooped up by Termite, who lifted his boxer off the canvas. The final score was 21-7. He'd done what his American sparring partner had not been able to accomplish – he'd won in the Olympics.

Leaving the ring, the media pressed against him. Iraqi officials immediately tried to push them away, but Termite stopped them. "Let him have his day," he admonished. A beaming Najah said to the media, "These are my coaches, I listened to them very much. I thank God for this win. This opened the door for Iraqi boxers in the next Olympics. There *will* be more boxers from Iraq." He was the tallest 106-pound man in the world that day, telling the reporters, "I just focused on what we trained on." It sounded so simple.

Najah and Termite went back to their room for something of critical importance – Najah had to call home to Iraq. "Dad, I won!" he said into the cell phone. Najah's father had seen the fight, "Najah, do you hear that?" and paused for Najah to hear. Guns were going off all over their village in Baghdad in celebration of his win. Rather than aimed in war, they were being shot into the air in honor of their Olympic boxer. Najah was so moved that he had brought so much pride to Iraq. Najah and his dad talked for a moment about his performance in the ring, "You looked great, son." No matter what else happened, he was an Olympic winner and would return a hero to his home and country.

Termite and Najah had four days to prepare for the next fight, which could put him in the medal round. He faced a much tougher opponent in Aleksan Nalbandyan, an Armenian boxer who was coaxed out of retirement for the Olympics. In his early thirties, he had a great deal more experience than Najah, and even trained out of Houston for a time. At 5'3", the height advantage over Najah was a real concern, but what troubled his coach was the difference in number of times in the ring. It was difficult to compensate for sheer experience in ten months of training.

Najah entered the crammed arena to a standing ovation. Termite didn't know much about the Armenian boxer, except that he loved to get his opponent on the ropes. After their cheek kissing ritual and "I love you's," Termite settled his boxer down. "Najah," his coach instructed in the corner before the first bell, "Throw straight punches and combinations and stay off the ropes."

Najah fought a great fight, but he got behind in points in the first round. Having to play catch-up, he continued to fight hard, and cut the Armenian in the third round. Blood spewed from a bad cut on his opponent's eye, and later his nose. Sensing a victory for the underdog Iraqi, the crowd chanted, "Ali, Ali!" The referees stopped the fight for a minute for the doctor to look at the Armenian. Termite held his breath, hoping that the fight would be called and Najah would have the win. The referee signaled for the fight to continue. The crowd's chants of "Ali, Ali!" pushed him on, and he fought his huge heart out. Najah, like every boxer who fought a great fight, thought he'd won. Termite knew that it was a close fight, but felt that Iraq's quest for an Olympic medal was over. Disappointed but immensely proud, he gave Najah a huge bear hug and lifted him up for the crowd, who continued chanting his name.

After the fight, a Japanese reporter asked the boxer, "Najah, how did it feel to lose?" Najah calmly responded, "I didn't lose." The perplexed reporter persisted, "How does it feel to be a loser in the biggest fight of your life?" Najah questioned him, "Did I lose?" The reporter said, "What do you mean?" Najah said, "I'm free, my country is free, I just represented my country in the Olympics, and the world loves me. Did I lose?" The reporter paused and understood, "No, you may be the biggest winner of the whole Olympics."

The sheer focus of the quest had left no corners in Termite's mind for goodbyes. Under Termite's strict supervision for almost a year, the coach encouraged Najah to have fun with the Iraqi soccer team and enjoy Athens. Najah pleaded, "Come and go with us, Termite." Termite had to pull away from him because their separation was imminent at this point, and probably of a long duration. It would break both of their hearts, and Termite knew that some fun with the athletes would insulate that fall for Najah.

Termite left the Olympics early. His mission accomplished, his contract with the Coalition was near expiration, and he had to face the reality of finding a job back in the States. The bigger reality was an emotional one; it was devastatingly difficult to leave Najah. In Termite's mind, the quicker they separated the easier it would be on his athlete. Termite pressed Najah to go out with his Iraqi buddies that night. The truth was that he didn't want Najah to watch him pack. It killed the coach to send his beloved boxer back to an uncertain future in Baghdad.

Around 4:00 A.M., Termite woke him. "Najah, I'm heading for the airport." Najah resisted, "I'll go with you to the airport, Termite." Termite refused, "No, Najah you stay and sleep." Termite sat on the edge of his boxer's bed. "Najah, it's been such a privilege and an honor to be your coach. You know that I love you, son." In the middle of the night in a huge dormitory village, two men who had nothing in common ten months ago, held tightly to each other. "Termite, "Najah said, "Thank you for everything, Termite. I love you. Neither wanted to be the first to release their grip on the other. "Goodbye, Najah," Termite whispered, thankful that the dim lights hid the moisture of his eyes.

Riding the Olympic Village bus to the front gate, Termite remembered something Najah had said to one of the reporters in Athens. "I want the world to see that we're all normal. I'm very normal." Described as ambassadors of peace, symbols of freedom, and even a publicity stunt, they were both just boxers. Boxers who had found each other in the middle of a war zone and embarked on a journey to see a freedom-starved country back in an Olympic boxing ring. Normal men who wanted the freedom, the right, to climb between the ropes of a boxing ring in Athens and represent a people desperate for some peace in their homeland.

Termite left his home to protect the freedom he cherished in his own country. The most unexpected thing

184

happened to him – he fell in love with the people of Iraq and was entrusted with twenty-four of their most important citizens, their boxing team. He took a stand for their freedom and future. He would have died for them; they would have easily done the same for their coach. They were all freedom fighters – men who were normal in their settings, but who had risen to the challenge. They'd followed a crazy, freedom-loving Texan on a "one chance in a million" quest and had accomplished the seemingly impossible. Freedom now burned in the hearts of those big-hearted boxers.

That fire, once lit, is inextinguishable and will spread throughout the country of Iraq. *Insha'Allah.*

Photo Courtesy of Cliff Roberts

January 30, 2005

The signs in Najah's village in Baghdad warned against voting in the strongest of words. "Vote and you'll die" was the basic theme repeated in Arabic on walls and flyers handed out to the people. Tribal meetings were held about the situation. Persecuted by Saddam Hussein for so many years, voting was a commodity so precious that they'd not deemed it possible until recently.

Walking past signs promising death to voters, Najah's family strode proudly into the Baghdad precinct to cast their ballots. As he told his American mentor on the phone after voting for the first time, "We're willing to die to vote." Iraq was still struggling with violence and uncertainty, but a powerful freedom had arrived. The act of checking off a candidate's name on a sheet of paper, something Americans often view as a hassle, brought profound feelings of joy for millions of Iraqis. They would determine their country's future, not a dictator surrounded by armed thugs.

Najah had not expected to still be in Iraq for the election. Accepted into the University of Houston to begin work on his master's degree, the fall and spring quarters passed without Najah. A bureaucratic stonewall in Greece stalled Termite's plan to continue Najah's training and education in Texas. Unequivocally certain that he will find a way, Termite continues working with state and national politicians to bring Najah to the United States. Najah continues to wait for that call.

188